PRAISE FOR

COLORBLIND: THE RISE OF POST-RACIAL POLITICS AND THE RETREAT FROM RACIAL EQUITY

"With *Colorblind*, Tim Wise offers a gutsy call to arms. Rather than play nice and reiterate the fiction of black racial transcendence, Wise takes the gloves off: He insists white Americans themselves must be at the forefront of the policy shifts necessary to correct our nation's racial imbalances in crime, health, wealth, education and more. A piercing, passionate and illuminating critique of the post-racial moment."

—Bakari Kitwana, author of *The Hip-Hop Generation: Young Blacks and the Crisis in African American Culture*

"Tim Wise's *Colorblind* brilliantly challenges the idea that the election of Obama has ushered in a post-racial era. In clear, engaging, and accessible prose, Wise explains that ignoring problems does not make them go away, that race-bound problems require race-conscious remedies. Perhaps most important, Colorblind proposes practical solutions to our problems and promotes new ways of thinking that encourage us to both recognize differences and to transcend them."

—George Lipsitz, author of *The Possessive Investment in Whiteness*

"At every turn and every corner, in every crevice and every crack, Tim Wise debunks the mythology of a 'color blind' society with the vigor of a statistician and the passion befitting one of the preeminent anti-racist theorists working today. You will literally lose your breath trying to keep up with the ways that Wise lays waste to the idea that we've achieved anything close to a 'post-race' society. If you don't know who Tim Wise is, you will after this book."

—Mark Anthony Neal, author of *New Black Man* and Professor of African & African-American Studies at Duke University

PRAISE FOR
BETWEEN BARACK AND A HARD PLACE

"Wise's short book reads like an old-school polemic: Thomas Paine's *Common Sense* for the 21st century. . . . A post-racial United States is an imagined country."

—*Washington Post*

"Wise, a white anti-racism activist and scholar (and author of *White Like Me*), pushes plenty of buttons in this methodical breakdown of racism's place in the wake of Barack Obama's victory. . . . There's no sugar coating here for whites, nor are there any news flashes for Americans of color, but Wise bravely enumerates the unpalatable truths of a nation still struggling to understand its legacy of racist oppression."

—*Publishers Weekly*

"Wise outlines . . . how racism and white privilege have morphed to fit the modern social landscape. In prose that reads like his lightning-rod speeches, he draws from a long list of high-profile campaign examples to define what he calls 'Racism 2.0,' a more insidious form of racism that actually allows for and celebrates the achievements of individual people of color because they're seen as the exceptions, not the rules."

—*Colorlines*

"This book makes an intriguing argument and is packed with insight. Wise clearly explains the complexity of institutional racism in contemporary society. He continuously reminds the reader that Obama's victory *may* signal the entrenchment of a more complicated, subtle, and insidious form of racism. The jury is still out."

—*Multicultural Review*

"Tim Wise has looked behind the curtain. In *Between Barack and a Hard Place* he explores the real issues of race in the Obama campaign and incoming presidency, issues that the mainstream media has chosen to ignore. His book debunks any notion that the United States has entered a post-racial period; instead he identifies the problems that emerge in the context of the victory of a black presidential candidate who chose to run an essentially non-racial campaign. With this book, Wise hits the bull's-eye."

—Bill Fletcher, Jr., Executive Editor of *BlackCommentator.com* and co-founder of the Center for Labor Renewal

PRAISE FOR TIM WISE

"Tim Wise is one of the most brilliant, articulate and courageous critics of white privilege in the nation. His considerable rhetorical skills, his fluid literary gifts and his relentless search for the truth make him a critical ally in the fight against racism and a true soldier in the war for social justice. His writing and thinking constitute a bulwark of common sense, and uncommon wisdom, on the subject of race, politics and culture. He is a national treasure."

—Michael Eric Dyson, University Professor,
Georgetown University

"(Wise's) work is revolutionary, and those who react negatively are simply afraid of hearing the truth. . . ."

—Robin D.G. Kelley, Professor of History, University of
Southern California

"Tim Wise is one of those rare 'public intellectuals' that numerous authors have suggested are becoming extinct in this society. He is evidence that this is not the case. . . . In my judgment, he is the very best of the white anti-racism writers and commentators working in the U.S. media today. . . ."

—Joe Feagin, Graduate Research Professor of
Sociology, Texas A&M

"One of the brilliant voices of our time."

—Molefi Kete Asante, Professor of African American
Studies, Temple University

"Wise is the nation's leading antiracist author/activist. . . ."
—David Naguib Pellow, professor of Ethnic Studies, University of Minnesota

"(His) is the clearest thinking on race I've seen in a long while written by a white writer . . . right up there with the likes of historians Howard Zinn and Herb Aptheker as far as I'm concerned."
—Dr. Joyce King, Benjamin E. Mays Endowed Chair for Urban Teaching, Learning and Leadership, Georgia State University

COLORBLIND

The Rise of Post-Racial Politics and the Retreat from Racial Equity

Tim Wise

CITY LIGHTS BOOKS / OPEN MEDIA SERIES
San Francisco

The Open Media Series is edited by Greg Ruggiero and archived by the Tamiment Library, New York University.

Cover design: Pollen

Library of Congress Cataloging-in-Publication Data
Wise, Tim J.
Colorblind : the rise of post-racial politics and the retreat from racial equity / Tim Wise.
p. cm. — (Open media series)
Includes bibliographical references.
ISBN 978-0-87286-508-2
1. United States—Race relations. 2. United States—Race relations—Political aspects. 3. Racism—Political aspects—United States. 4. Liberalism—United States. 5. African Americans—Civil rights—History—20th century. I. Title. II. Series.

E185.615.W557 2010
305.800973—dc22

2010006545

City Lights Books are published at City Lights Bookstore
261 Columbus Avenue, San Francisco, CA 94133
www.citylights.com

Contents

Preface

"There's not a liberal America and a conservative America; there's the United States of America. There's not a black America and a white America and Latino America and Asian America; there's the United States of America."

With these words, delivered as part of his first speech to a national audience, then–Illinois state senator Barack Obama elicited uproarious applause from those assembled in Boston for the 2004 Democratic National Convention. As political theater goes, it was nearly perfect, not only for dyed-in-the-wool party faithful, but for a nation largely unfamiliar with the young U.S. Senate candidate. In the span of approximately a half-hour, Obama straddled the line between liberal platitudes and moderate-to-conservative bombast, calling for studious adherence to civil liberties in the midst of the so-called "war on terror," but also insisting that the United States had enemies that must be found, pursued "and defeated." On the domestic front, this ideological ecumenism continued, with Obama calling for substantial public investments in health care and education, apropos for most any liberal politician, and then turning rightward, emphasizing the importance of self-reliance and personal responsibility in the face of hardship. To that end, he called for parents to turn off the television and, in what seemed like a broadside directed specifically at the African American community, admonished black folks to reject the oft lamented (but according to scholarly research, over-claimed) mentality that to be "black with a book" is to be guilty of "acting white." In short, there was something in the speech for most everyone.

Although Obama said little during his keynote that evening about race or racism, he stood before the nation (and the world) as a living embodiment of America's longstanding racial drama. As he discussed his ancestry—his Kenyan father and Kansas-born mother—he seemed to suggest that his very presence on the stage was symbolic of something larger than himself, and surely larger than Senator John Kerry, whom he had come to praise that night as the Party's candidate for president. Indeed, Obama made a point of claiming that "in no other country on Earth" was his story "even possible." Presumably, there was something uniquely good, and uniquely multicultural, about the United States. Despite our long night of the soul when it comes to race, and the legacy of white supremacy from which the country was only beginning to emerge at the time of Obama's birth, the young and charismatic orator assured us, we were well on our way to the Promised Land. His own life story was proof of it.

To the commentators who make up what we might call the *cognitariat* of American politics, Obama was a blessing on two fronts: first, a political figure with a polish and youthful vitality unseen since John F. Kennedy; and second, a man of color who despite his racial identity seemed at home in the center of the political spectrum, largely unconnected to civil rights and antiracist movements, and unthreatening to whites who had long ago turned off to identifiably black political struggles and leaders. He quickly became the darling of the chattering class: a bunch that was mostly white, well educated (and thus taken with his Harvard Law pedigree), and politically center-left, much like this new upstart from Chicago.

Though most predicted a bright future for Obama, few could have expected the trajectory his life would take within four short years. It is, after all, one thing to have your book rise to the top of the best-seller list, or even to win a Grammy Award (as Obama did, for the audio version of his autobiography), but it is quite another to become president of the United States. Yet he managed to do just that—beating Senator John McCain even before completing his own first term in the U.S. Senate—to become the nation's first black president.

Obama won the White House with a combination of deft political strategy and the enthusiasm of millions of young people, energized by his persona and by his relative generational proximity to them. Obama was the candidate of college students, recent graduates and those between 30 and 45. Senator McCain was "your grandfather's" candidate: the former POW, a fighter from an older era (both chronologically and in terms of disposition). In an age defined by media imagery, Obama's win should have come as no surprise. Yet right up until the end, there was doubt about his ability to prevail. Yes, he was the far better spoken candidate. Yes, he had the more detailed policy positions. Yes, he had lots of money—more than his opponent—and some of the best political minds behind him. Yes, he was running against a party that had given the nation George W. Bush, whose policies, by 2008, were fiercely unpopular. And yes, he had all those young people. But still, there was the question of race.

Put simply, how could a nation founded as a white settler colony built with the forced labor of enslaved Africans—and where whites were still the majority of voters—elect a man of color less than two generations after the fall of formal apartheid? For some, the answer was simple: *It couldn't*. Whites might say they were going to support Obama, but in the end, they would pull the lever for McCain. That was the conventional wisdom for many, polls notwithstanding. But despite the naysayers, the senator trudged on, picking up unexpected levels of support even in traditionally conservative states, leaving the pundits to scratch their heads and ask if there had been some political realignment about which they had been theretofore unaware. Could it be that white Americans had finally overcome their biases, such that they might now elect a black president? And not just any black president, but one with the middle name *Hussein*?

The results of the election are now history. President Obama, though he received fewer than half of all white votes cast, did manage to obtain more white votes than any Democrat in the previous forty-plus years. But what that outcome says and doesn't say about white racial bias is less clear. Indeed, in my last book, *Between Barack and a Hard Place: Racism and White Denial in the Age of Obama*, I document the extent of ongoing racial discrimination in the United States, and the significant degree to which white Americans, by their own admission, continue to adhere to a number of fundamentally racist views about African Americans and other people of color. Therein, I suggest that Obama's election, far from serving as evidence that racism had been defeated, might signal a mere shape-shifting of racism, from Racism 1.0 to Racism 2.0, an insidious upgrade that allows millions of whites to cling to racist stereotypes about people of color generally, while nonetheless carving out exceptions for those who, like Obama, make us comfortable by seeming so "different" from what we view as a much less desirable norm.

In *Colorblind*, I examine more closely the consequences of the Obama victory, in terms of its likely long-term effects on the nation's racial discourse. Where *Between Barack and a Hard Place* sought to explore what the election said, and didn't say, about racism in America, *Colorblind* examines the impact of the Obama victory on our ability as a nation to tackle—or even openly discuss—matters of race and racism.

Principally, I seek to explore what is perhaps the most disturbing dilemma of the current political moment as regards matters of race. On the one hand, it was candidate Obama's use of the *rhetoric of racial transcendence* that made his victory possible, by assuaging white fears that he would focus on racial injustice, or seek to remedy the same, were he elected president. But on the other hand, it is that same avoidance of race issues that has now made it more difficult than ever to address ongoing racial bias, and has hamstrung the president's ability to push back against some of the opposition to his agenda, even when that opposition is framed in blatantly racist ways. Furthermore, because the rhetoric of racial transcendence requires a similarly race-neutral policy agenda to match it, Obama has eschewed any direct focus on narrowing racial gaps in income, wealth, education, housing or health care, in favor of a "universal" approach that purports to help all in need. While such efforts may disproportionately benefit persons of color—if simply because they are disproportionately among those at the bottom of the socioeconomic hierarchy—they are presented to the masses as the product of colorblind public policy.

This combination of race-neutral rhetoric and colorblind public policy comprise what I call *post-racial liberalism*. Post-racial liberalism is a form of left-of-center politics, which has had its adherents dating back at least forty years, and which emerged after the civil rights revolution had largely accomplished its immediate goals with the passage of legal protections against discrimination in employment and public accommodations (1964), voting (1965) and housing (1968). In the wake of those legislative victories, and following several years of violent uprisings in urban centers thanks to frustration at the slow pace of change—especially with regard to economic opportunity—some of the nation's scholars and public intellectuals began to turn against race-specific remedies for lingering racial inequities. Beginning in the late 1970s with sociologist William Julius Wilson's *The Declining Significance of Race* and extending through to the Obama campaign for the presidency, post-racial liberalism has advocated a de-emphasis of racial discrimination and race-based remedies for inequality, in favor of class-based or "universal" programs of uplift: from job creation policies to better education funding to health care reform.

In *Colorblind*, I explore the rise of post-racial liberalism, culminating in the election of Barack Obama as president in 2008. Obama's victory, dependent as it was on a rhetoric of racial transcendence and a public policy agenda of colorblind universalism, can be seen as the ultimate triumph for the post-racial approach.

In chapter one, we'll examine the way in which Obama represents and extends the tradition of post-racial liberalism, in terms of his rhetoric and public policy stance. Then in chapter two, we'll explore the potential consequences of post-racial liberalism for the cause of racial justice and the reasons why post-racial liberalism is problematic, few of which have been explored publicly since Obama's election.

First, post-racial liberalism is inadequate for remedying persistent racial inequities. Because those inequities are themselves too often the result of racial discrimination and race-specific injuries perpetrated by whites against people of color—and not, as post-racial liberalism insists, the result of race-neutral economic or cultural factors—applying "universal" solutions to said inequities will likely fail to fully ameliorate them. Even the pragmatic case made for colorblind universalism—namely, that it is the only approach that can garner white support for progressive social policy—is of dubious validity. Because of a steady drumbeat of racially coded conservative propaganda concerning government programs for those in need, even universal public policy approaches (with regard to education, health care or job creation) will likely be seen as disproportionately benefiting people of color. This in turn will trigger white racial resentment, which is regularly manipulated by reactionary commentators and politicians seeking to derail the Obama presidency. Hence, to ignore race and push a race-blind rhetoric and policy approach will only allow the right to manipulate racial angers unmolested and unchecked. In other words, the notion that liberals' post-racial approach will allow for the building of political support for progressive policies rests on a naïve understanding of how the public *perceives* social policy, even when it is presented in terms that are colorblind. To the extent that much of the white public envisions such efforts as universal health care, job creation or increased educational funding as efforts intended to help people of color, post-racial liberalism will fail, even on its own terms.

Secondly, implicit racial biases (which often exist side-by-side with an outwardly non-racist demeanor and persona) frequently influence the way we view and treat others. Being aware of these biases and alert to their possible triggering gives us all a fighting chance at keeping them in check. But colorblindness, by discouraging discussions of racial matters and presuming that the best practice is to ignore the realities of racism, makes it more difficult to challenge those biases, and thus increases the likelihood of discrimination. To the extent a public discourse of colorblindness "trickles down" to our private lives, workplaces, schools and elsewhere, thereby discouraging us from taking race and its consequences into account, we will likely fail to adequately address real and persistent racial bias and fail to ensure true equity of opportunity.

In fact, as I will argue, colorblindness not only fails to remedy discrimination and racial inequity, it can actually make both problems worse. To begin, if the rhetoric of racial transcendence gives the impression—as it does, almost by definition—that the racial injustices of the past are no longer instrumental in determining life chances and outcomes, it will become increasingly likely that persons seeing significant racial stratification in society will rationalize those disparities as owing to some cultural or biological flaw on the part of those at the bottom of the hierarchy. In other words, racial bias would become almost *rational* once observers of inequity were deprived of the critical social context needed to understand the conditions they observe. Whereas a color-conscious approach allows for a more nuanced understanding of racial inequities and how they've been generated, colorblindness encourages placing blame for the conditions of inequity on those who have been the targets of systemic injustice. Ironically, this means that colorblindness, often encouraged as the ultimate non-racist mentality, might have the consequence of giving new life to racist thinking.

Additionally, colorblindness can perpetuate and even deepen systemic racism. Encouraging individuals and institutions to downplay the role of race and racism in the lives of the public will only impede the ability to respond to the needs of that public. For instance, if employers operate on the basis of colorblindness, they will be less likely to consider the way that job applicants of color have been impacted by the opportunity structure; so too admissions officers at colleges and universities. Thus they may perceive applicants of color as less qualified than their white counterparts, based solely on a handful of outward manifestations of merit, which are themselves heavily influenced by that opportunity structure. Whereas color-conscious approaches allow and even encourage institutions to take into consideration the full range of factors that might shape a job or college applicant's on-paper credentials (and thus engage in deliberate efforts to provide opportunity to those who may have less impressive formal resumes but be equally or more qualified), colorblindness makes it unlikely that such considerations would be brought to bear.

In the final analysis, the problem with colorblindness and post-racial liberalism is that they ignore the different ways in which we experience the society around us. If certain people face obstacles not faced by others—such as race-based discrimination—then universal programs of general uplift cannot possibly serve as the palliative for their condition. Likewise, imagine how absurd it would be to say that universal programs of opportunity were the best solution for persons who were disabled. Since persons with disabilities face obstacles that are directly related to their disability—including presumptions of lesser competence and actual physical constraints in workplaces and elsewhere—to think that economic growth alone, or a jobs bill, or universal health care would suffice to remedy their social disempowerment would be preposterous. So much so that no one would ever offer universal solutions for improving life for the disabled, or an "ability-blind" approach, since to be blind to (dis)ability is to make it impossible to address the very thing that is giving rise to the individual's mistreatment and lesser opportunity in the first place.

By endorsing colorblind universalism as a solution to persistent inequities, President Obama implies, intentionally or not, that there are no institutional obstacles faced by people of color that could not be weakened or abolished by colorblind policies and programs alone. He also implies that whites and people of color face the same set of obstacles and do so on a relatively even playing field. But these notions are so utterly saturated with falsehood that a man as intelligent as he simply cannot believe them, which then leaves only political calculation as the basis for his position. Sadly, if President Obama is willing to ignore the pain of race-based discrimination and injustice, so as to make whites comfortable—and this, after he has already been elected and the campaign is long over—then the likelihood he will ever speak the truth about these matters, let alone address them, shrinks to nearly zero. In which case there is no option left but for us to correct the record, and pointedly, before his approach does real damage to the cause of civil rights and racial equity.

In the final chapter, I propose a new paradigm for both public policy considerations and private personal and institutional practice: an approach I call *illuminated individualism.* While conservatives have long pushed for a complete disregarding of group identity in favor of a focus on rugged individualism and personal achievement, and liberals like Obama have promoted a collective national identity under a "one America" motif, herein I suggest a third option. Illuminated individualism seeks to respect the uniqueness of all persons and communities—and thus not to assume that racial identity or country of origin, as in the case of non-citizens seeking to become residents, automatically tells us what we need to know about a person and their background—while yet acknowledging the general truth that to be white, a person of color, indigenous, or an immigrant continues to have meaning in the United States.

In other words, we are neither *merely* individuals, nor merely Americans. Race continues to matter. Only by being aware of that meaning and resolving to view individuals and communities as they really are—which requires acknowledging their languages, cultures, traditions, and racialized experiences—can we actually hope to build the kind of democracy that treats all persons fairly and equally. And just as important, only by illuminating our own individual and community uniqueness—including our personal biases—can we hope to check the tendency to disadvantage and exclude, which sadly is still far too common. Illuminated individualism then suggests a number of policy options and practices, at both the public and private level, which I also explore in this concluding chapter.

Although there is certainly much political activity on the right that concerns me, merely critiquing the often overtly racist machinations of reactionaries is insufficient for a political moment such as this. Just as important, those committed to a truly equitable nation must explore the ways in which our responses to right-wing rhetoric and race-baiting have often been ill informed. Indeed, efforts by those on the right to roll back many of the gains that have been hard-fought over the years when it comes to racial equity are only enhanced by post-racial liberalism and the politics of colorblindness. In effect, post-racial liberalism gives aid and comfort to the right-wing enemy, and must be fought directly as the enabling force that it has come to be. If those of us committed to racial justice (and this would include people who consider themselves liberals, progressives, leftists, radicals, and even many so-called moderates) would challenge colorblindness and make the case for color-consciousness and racism-consciousness, we might yet build and strengthen the social movements needed to repel attacks from those who deliberately seek to weaken the freedom struggle.

Although there are many arenas in which racism perpetrated by whites continues to manifest, I have chosen here to focus on four specific areas: employment, housing, education and health care. Previously I have written about racism in the justice system, and I consider this to be a vitally important area for exploration. But in this book I have chosen not to examine racism in the criminal justice system, principally because unlike with the other subjects, there is no significant post-racial liberal approach to resolve the disparities in terms of sentencing, profiling or punishment. Most all folks to the left of the political spectrum, when they address racism in the justice system, endorse, at least in theory, race-conscious bans on racial profiling, and attention to race-specific disparities in sentencing, particularly regarding drug incarcerations. In other words, there is no real colorblind universal approach to addressing racial disparity in the justice system, as there is with the other areas of consideration. Since this volume seeks to critique a particular school of thought, I have chosen to focus my efforts on those arenas of life where the president and others have put forward a clear articulation of post-racial liberalism and colorblind universalism: jobs, housing, schooling and health. For those interested in the evidence regarding justice system bias, the data in *Between Barack and a Hard Place* is, unfortunately, still pertinent and worth examining.

Because of my use of the term "colorblind" in the title, and the repeated reference to the problems of colorblindness throughout this book, I would be remiss if I didn't at least reference the work of sociologist Eduardo Bonilla-Silva, whose concept of "colorblind racism" has been so helpful in shaping the last several years of critical race theory and analysis. In Bonilla-Silva's work, the term colorblind racism refers to the dominant white racial ideology of the modern era, in which whites, under the guise of being colorblind, refuse to acknowledge the reality of racism and reject any consideration of how their own racial identity provides them with privileges vis-à-vis people of color. By taking a stance amounting to that of a 3-year-old who sticks his fingers in his ears and shouts "la, la, la, la" over and over again to avoid hearing whatever his parents might be saying, many whites evade race as a topic, thereby allowing them to cast as racist anyone who broaches the subject. Colorblind racism supports white perspectives that people of color are to blame for their own problems in life—after all, if we're being colorblind we don't examine the historical structures of white domination that so often determine social position—and thereby deepens white racial hostility to the very people of color about whom whites are technically resolving not to think of in racialized and bigoted ways. This book examines the notion of colorblind racism in a slightly different way than Bonilla-Silva, exploring its operation within the national political discourse and the way in which it stems from a longer tradition of post-racial liberalism dating back decades.

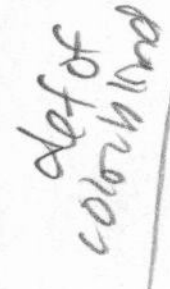

Although *Colorblind* takes aim at a form of modern liberalism, the critique of colorblindness contained herein is meant for anyone, regardless of self-professed political ideology, who believes that paying *less* attention to race and racial identity is the proper response to racial inequity. This includes many liberals, to be sure, but also some who are further to the left and who, because of their focus on economic class, occasionally give short shrift to race and racism as well. So too, persons who would never consider themselves on the left at all, per se, but who fervently believe, often with the best of intentions, that colorblindness is a positive paradigm for thought and action. It is my hope that even if, at the end of the day, readers disagree about the political efficacy of colorblind public policy, they will yet re-commit themselves in their private and professional lives to a more color-conscious direction, so as to foster greater equity of opportunity throughout the institutional spaces where we all operate.

I would like to thank my editor, Greg Ruggiero, for his encouragement and patience with me as I prepared this manuscript, despite a grueling lecture schedule for the past several months.

Also, my thanks to Elaine, Stacey, and everyone at City Lights Books for their support of my work. And of course, special thanks to my wife, Kristy, and our two daughters, Ashton and Rachel, whose constant love and encouragement are what truly sustain me and make possible any and all of my accomplishments.

Nashville, Tennessee
March 2010

ONE

The Rise and Triumph of Post-Racial Liberalism

In 1970, Daniel Patrick Moynihan—scholar, advisor to Presidents Johnson and Nixon, and later a United States senator—called for the initiation of a period of "benign neglect" regarding racial matters in America. After more than a decade of intense focus on racism, both in the media and political realm—extending from the Montgomery bus boycott to the passage of the Voting Rights Act to fair housing legislation in 1968—some Democrats, including Moynihan, had come to believe that it was time for a respite from the subject. As whites became increasingly agitated about urban riots during the middle and latter part of the sixties, these voices began to argue that in order for the nation to move forward on an agenda of opportunity for all, it would be necessary to de-emphasize the issue of racism and discrimination, and focus instead on other concerns.

For Moynihan, this meant examining what he viewed as an internal cultural crisis in black America, exemplified by an increase in single-parent homes, criminal violence in cities and an inadequate attachment to dominant social norms and mores. Although Moynihan, like most liberals, allowed that these distressing cultural developments in the black family and community had structural roots—they were not, in other words, indicative of something inherently flawed in black culture itself—the tone of his criticism, which had been embodied in a 1965 document that has come to be known as "The Moynihan Report on the Black Family," suggested that the problems of the black community could no longer be solved by way of social policies aimed at addressing racism.[1] In Moynihan's report, one could find data indicating growing rates of out-of-wedlock childbirth and familial breakdown, as well as presumed welfare dependency among African Americans. To Moynihan, family breakdown could explain most of the problems seen in low-income communities of color, rather than a history of unjust treatment, let alone discrimination in the present.

In line with this thinking—itself part of an emerging "culture of poverty" analysis—Moynihan also suggested that whatever attempts were made to directly address inequity at the systemic level would need to be race-neutral. At a public forum sponsored by the American Academy of Arts and Sciences in 1965, Moynihan articulated the political imperative of colorblind universalism.[2] There, he proclaimed that although he viewed the problems faced by low-income blacks to be different from the problems faced by other poor people, for political reasons it would likely be necessary to reject targeted efforts aimed at addressing those unique problems, in favor of programs that sought to uplift all in need. He noted, for instance, that anti-poverty efforts then under way as part of the Great Society initiative had been colorblind, and thus had received more political support than otherwise would have been the case.

As Moynihan put it: "Congressmen vote for everyone more readily than they vote for any one," a sentiment he would then follow with a criticism of compensatory or preferential treatment for blacks (as with what would come to be known as affirmative action efforts). In other words, for political reasons, Moynihan supported an early form of post-racial liberalism.

Though the Great Society programs had indeed been race-neutral—and in this Moynihan, who had been involved in their drafting, was correct—they certainly have not come to be remembered or perceived as such more than forty years on: an important point, the implications of which we'll explore a bit later. Indeed, even by the 1970s, much of the so-called war on poverty was already being remembered, and lambasted, as a gigantic handout scheme for urban blacks. As conservative politicians increasingly sought to scapegoat welfare efforts for everything from taxes to crime to family dissolution, they relied on an ever-intensifying racial narrative with regard to those programs. The imagery they conjured as they attacked liberal social policy was explicitly racialized.[3] In this they were aided by mass media that, beginning in the early 1970s, shifted the racial composition of their representations of poor people from mostly white to mostly black and brown.[4] As the imagery changed, so did white attitudes toward anti-poverty efforts, however "universal" they may have been in practice. By the 1980s, conservatives had done a masterful job of linking several race-sensitive issues in the white imagination, among them welfare spending, busing for the purpose of school desegregation, and affirmative action efforts.

COLORBLIND UNIVERSALISM AND PUBLIC POLICY

In the wake of a brewing white backlash to what some perceived as the "excesses" of the 1960s, some scholars, even liberal ones, began to revisit the Moynihan Report, if not its specific focus on black family decay, at least its support for neglecting racism as an issue, in favor of a different focus. Although these liberal voices rarely joined the conservative chorus that was calling for the literal rolling back of certain civil rights era gains, they did propose a move away from race-focused analysis and public policy: again, benign neglect, in Moynihan's terms, rather than its more malignant conservative counterpart.

And so it was that in 1978 sociologist William Julius Wilson, initially of the University of Chicago and later Harvard, penned his influential and award-winning book *The Declining Significance of Race*. Therein, he encouraged policy makers to look away from racial discrimination in order to understand conditions of life for black Americans. Rather, Wilson insisted, we can find the reasons for those conditions in largely race-neutral, structural economic changes such as the collapse of manufacturing jobs or inadequate funding for education.[5] He would follow this up in 1987 with *The Truly Disadvantaged*, which made largely the same arguments as his earlier effort.

Interestingly, as sociologist Stephen Steinberg notes, Wilson originally considered titling this second book "The Hidden Agenda," by which he was referring to the necessity of hiding programs aimed at helping blacks behind a veil of colorblind universalism. Wilson apparently felt the need for such subterfuge due to a belief that there would be little political support, especially from whites, for efforts to uplift people of color. That Wilson recognized white antipathy towards race-specific efforts was, in a sense, the ultimate irony, in that it suggested that far from being of "declining" significance, race was still a major determiner of political ideology and perspective. For whites, any attempts at addressing persistent racial inequality would be resisted, if it were understood that such a goal was intended. Steinberg commented on the contradiction in Wilson's position:

> Indeed, it is *because* of racism that Wilson feels compelled to "hide" his agenda in the first place. The underlying premise is that America is *so* racist—so utterly indifferent to the plight of black America, so implacably opposed to any indemnification for three centuries of racial oppression—that it becomes necessary to camouflage policies intended for blacks behind policies that offer benefits to the white majority.[6]

In *The Truly Disadvantaged*, Wilson advanced two principal positions. First, he claimed that the plight of the black poor is mostly about a spatial mismatch between where such persons live and where new jobs are being created. Because of the decline of manufacturing in urban centers and the shift to service-sector jobs that are often located in suburbs, blacks are simply locked out of opportunities. Racism is no longer the problem, according to Wilson; rather, blacks are now the victims of geography and race-neutral macroeconomic transformations. In keeping with this diagnosis, Wilson puts forward his second principal claim: that the solution to the economic plight of African Americans and their communities would be a massive New Deal–type effort intended to provide opportunity to all who are economically marginalized. He avers therein that such an effort will be of greatest relative benefit to the urban poor of color, but by virtue of helping all who need assistance, be politically more palatable than race-targeted measures.[7]

Although Wilson offered no evidence to bolster his claim that manufacturing layoffs had been sufficient to explain the plight of inner city blacks, nor to demonstrate that black folks' inability to land service-sector jobs was about spatial isolation (as opposed to, say, the racism of service-sector employers), his conclusions were celebrated and accepted as conventional wisdom by many. Among Wilson's supporters was one Bill Clinton, who as president credited Wilson with informing his own understanding of race and class issues.[8]

So too, scholars like Wilson joined many on the right in conjuring the image of cultural pathology in so-called ghetto communities and suggesting that many of the problems faced therein stemmed more from self-destructive adaptations to centuries of injustice, rather than to the injustices themselves. Whereas the right-wing version of this "culture of poverty" thesis tended to be militantly judgmental, even racist—in that it came close to suggesting there was something essential about black culture that tended towards pathology—the liberal version offered by Wilson tried to

be more forgiving. Yes, Wilson would note, enslavement and segregation were the root causes of those pathologies we could now see in urban communities—from broken families to educational failure to crime—but unless those pathologies were seen as free-standing contributors to black folks' current plight, there would be little chance of improving the conditions of life for people suffering under their weight.

And thus, by the late 1980s, post-racial liberalism was in full swing, having now been joined and even led by a black scholar in Wilson, giving it a patina of respectability that it may never have enjoyed had only whites like Moynihan crafted it. Though Wilson was its first and brightest star, others would join him over the years, some white and others black. Though they differed on the specifics, the common thread of their work has been that for reasons of political practicality, progressive social policy needs to focus less on race, racism and injustice directed at blacks and other persons of color, and more on "universal" programs of uplift regarding jobs, education, healthcare and other arenas of daily life. Far from abandoning the fight against inequality itself, these thinkers—from Jim Sleeper to Richard Kahlenberg to Stanford law professor Richard Thompson Ford, most recently[9]—propose two things: first, that the best way to get at persistent inequities is to focus on causes for them that are more about economics than race per se, and second, that in order to build any kind of political momentum for progressive policy, a switch from race-focused to class-focused or universal efforts will likely be needed.

Although Wilson claims to have rethought his earlier dismissal of the role of racism in explaining conditions faced by African Americans—largely because of field research he and his students conducted in Chicago, during which employers made blatantly racist comments to explain their refusal to hire black men—his most recent book, *More Than Just Race*, still focuses principally on the need for universal and colorblind remedies for problems that beset the urban poor of color. Even in the section of *More Than Just Race* that purports to address race-specific barriers faced by blacks, evidence of racism and discrimination (which has been amply provided by scholars in Wilson's own field for years, and will be examined later in this volume) is almost entirely ignored.

Not only is Wilson loath to document discrimination in his newest work; he is also extraordinarily quick to excuse it, even when he is the target. So, for instance, he finesses the reaction of white residents to his own black presence in his condominium complex. Though their apparent nervousness when encountering Wilson in casual dress might be chalked up to racism, he notes it may simply be an understandable reaction to seeing a black man in street clothes, given media portrayals of black men, crime and rates of disproportionate black criminality.[10] That Wilson can define this kind of thinking as something other than racism—as if somehow racism *isn't* what a person is guilty of when they extrapolate to each black person in casual clothes the deviance of a statistical minority—is stunning, and suggests that whatever he may have learned about racism during that research in Chicago, there is still a considerable amount—including, say, the very definition of the term—that eludes him.

For all his vaunted rediscovery of racism, Wilson still pays far less attention to that subject than the long-shopworn platitudes about black cultural pathology and "lifestyle" choices, which have been a staple of his work for three decades. In fact, he continues to brag about his presumed bravery in addressing cultural pathology, calling his own willingness to do so "daring," even though it has been central to conservative and even much liberal thought on race and poverty since the mid-1960s.[11] Though Wilson ultimately comes down on the side of focusing attention on structural change rather than cultural change within the black community—and so, as always, remains a liberal exponent of culture-of-poverty thinking rather than a reactionary expositor of the same—the analysis he offers, and the public policies he endorses, continue to sound much like the ones he advocated in *The Truly Disadvantaged*. He is still proposing colorblind universalism and is an active agent of the politics of post-racial liberalism.

So, for instance, in his recitation of the problem facing blacks structurally, he continues to stress the shift in employment from urban manufacturing to suburban-based service-sector jobs: the exact argument he was making thirty years ago. And as with those previous efforts, he mentions the way that blacks in the cities are largely locked out of those jobs because of "spatial mismatch."[12] But as he has done for the past three decades, Wilson largely fails to connect the dots between racism and the creation of that mismatch in the first place. The fact is, there would be no spatial mismatch had race not for so long determined where blacks were allowed to live. It is a history of racial discrimination and preferential housing opportunities by and for whites that is to blame for whatever geographic "mismatch" Wilson manages to now identify.

Hundreds of thousands of homes and apartments lived in by folks of color (amounting to about one-fifth of all black and brown housing) were destroyed from the 1950s to the late 1960s, thanks to so-called "urban renewal," and this occurred at the same time whites were being subsidized by FHA loans and highway construction to move to the suburbs (and were successfully able to block blacks from moving there).[13] While Wilson mentions some of this in a later chapter of *More Than Just Race*, he doesn't directly connect that history—as well as ongoing discrimination—to the issue of job mismatch. Nor does he seem to think that efforts to attack and undo housing discrimination might be among the ways to address the spatial mismatch dilemma.

It is not that Wilson's arguments about macroeconomic forces and their effects on the urban poor of color are wrong, of course. But they are horribly incomplete. It is this problem of telling only a partial truth—that economic inequality is a serious problem with disproportionate impacts on people of color—that demarcates the boundaries of post-racial liberalism: a philosophy that seems to hold, inexplicably, that one can either support public policy aimed directly at reducing racial disparity or public policy intended to benefit everyone, but not both.

BARACK OBAMA AND THE RHETORIC OF RACIAL TRANSCENDENCE

It was post-racial liberalism that Barack Obama would carry forth into the political arena, beginning in 2004 at the Democratic National Convention, and that animated the applause line during his keynote speech about the country not being "a black America and white America and Latino America and Asian America," but rather, "the United States of America." And it was an approach largely mirrored in his books, from his memoir, *Dreams from My Father*, in which Obama wrestled with the uneasy legacy of his racial identity, bestowed upon him by an African father he would barely know, to his policy-themed offering, *The Audacity of Hope*. Especially in the latter, Obama evinced a clear desire to downplay racism as a subject and to balance out any discussions of it with statements intended to remind the reader that things were getting better, that black folks were often their own worst enemies, and that we were really all in the same boat.

On page 10 of *Audacity*, for instance, Obama allows that, obviously, he views the world through the lens of a black man, and that race continues to play a role in the life of the nation. Yet one page later, as if trying to insulate himself against a charge of being *too* race-sensitive, he makes clear the dangers of basing one's politics solely on racial identity. Although the notion that blacks see all issues through the prism of race is largely a white-constructed myth, Obama here seems to see the need to signal to white readers that he is not, at heart, as focused on race as earlier black community organizers, political leaders and activists. Thus he insists that "much of what ails the inner city involves a breakdown in culture," as if to suggest that whatever role race and racism may still play, much of the wound is self-inflicted.[14]

That Obama here morphs two issues into one—racism and poverty—when they are not the same, is hardly surprising. It has been a common trope of post-racial liberalism from the beginning: pay homage to the stark history of racism, then switch gears and ruminate on how the problems of poor people in so-called ghettos are now distant from the mistreatment that so often met their ancestors. That racial discrimination by whites might still be a problem for black and brown folks who are not at all poor escapes consideration altogether. It is as if poor = black and black = poor, in a bitter and ironclad equation, which permits no evaluation of the effects of this faulty claim, both on poor folks of all colors and persons of color in all socioeconomic strata.

Later in *Audacity*, Obama refuses to judge the founders of the nation too harshly, in spite of the hypocrisy that allowed them to preach democracy while enshrining slavery as an institution and even, in many cases, practicing it themselves. And so he explains that he cannot "choose sides" in the historical dispute between those who judge the founders lacking for their inconsistency, and those who choose to venerate them for having fashioned a Constitution that would one day be used to extend rights to persons of color. As with so many things, Obama tries to see both sides, and in the process blurs our ability to confront the magnitude of the founding crimes of the nation's white elites. After praising those he nonetheless calls "cranks," "zealots" and "the unreasonable"—referring to "unbending idealists" like abolitionist leader Frederick Douglass, and "wild-eyed" prophets like John Brown—he ultimately cannot join them in their idealism, their bravery, or their unyielding commitment to justice. In the end, as he puts it, he is "left with Lincoln" as a hero and role model. And why? Precisely because of his ability to balance his idealism with "practicality."[15]

Indeed, Lincoln was a pragmatist; so much so that he ultimately realized that sending black folks back to Africa—an idea he endorsed personally both before and after his election—was an unworkable plan, and thus not to be contemplated further. In fact, Lincoln even hedged on the issue of ending slavery. In the midst of the Civil War he wrote, "If I could save the Union, without freeing the slaves, I would do it. If I could do it by freeing some and leaving others alone, I would do that. What I do about slavery and the coloured race, I do because I believe it would help to save the Union." That Obama could eschew uncompromising anti-slavery fighters like Frederick Douglass, Harriet Tubman and John Brown for the likes of Abraham Lincoln says something. It suggests he is far more comfortable with that uneasy pragmatism, even in the face of considerable racism, the likes of which Lincoln surely endorsed. Although Obama wistfully says he would "like to believe that for Lincoln it was never a matter of abandoning conviction for the sake of expediency," one wonders to what extent he feels truly confident about that awkwardly stated hope.

Obama's willingness to praise the leadership of white presidents, despite their racial politics, does not end with Lincoln. Further in *Audacity*, he showers praise upon liberal social policy beginning with the New Deal initiatives of the Franklin Roosevelt administration.[16] Obama often speaks of the importance of the "social safety net" put in place during the New Deal, and during his 2004 keynote to the Democratic National Convention he made reference to how important those policies (and other economic opportunity efforts) had been to his own family, specifically, to his white grandparents.[17] This is important, given the way in which those efforts—though claimed as universal in scope and often credited with creating the American middle class—were actually intensely racialized.

From Social Security to the Federal Housing Administration's home loan program to later efforts like the GI Bill, white senators from the South saw to it that blacks would be largely excluded from these initiatives by way of the rules and regulations drawn up to govern their implementation: an exclusion that, in the case of Social Security, wouldn't be corrected for twenty years.[18] Indeed, President Roosevelt even refused to support an anti-lynching law for fear that Southern senators whose votes he needed to pass New Deal legislation might oppose him.[19] In other words, when Obama praises the New Deal, he is praising an effort that for all of its benefits—and they were many—essentially left people of color out in the cold. That he would fail to note this inherent flaw of such programs speaks to the way in which he deploys the rhetoric of racial transcendence and colorblindness: by downplaying the role of racism and discrimination, even when that role has been blatant. When Obama insists that "FDR recognized that we would all be more likely to take risks in our lives . . . if we knew that we would have some measure of protection should we fail," he essentially writes out of history the fact that FDR and his contemporaries did not, indeed, seek to provide those measures of protection for everyone.[20] When Obama uses the pronoun "we" in that comment, he is, by definition, identifying himself with whites in America, and not with persons of color.

In the section of *Audacity* dealing specifically with race, though Obama certainly notes the legacy of racism as a contributor to the current inequities between whites and people of color, he quickly turns to generic, universal programs of uplift as the remedy for those inequities about which he is concerned. Nowadays, Obama claims:

> . . . what ails working-class and middle-class blacks and Latinos is not fundamentally different from what ails their white counterparts: downsizing, outsourcing, automation,

> wage stagnation, the dismantling of employer-based health care and pension plans, and schools that fail to teach young people the skills they need to compete in a global economy.[21]

Starting from this diagnosis—which is dishonest, in that what ails people of color is not the same as what ails working-class and middle-class whites, since the latter don't face bigotry and discrimination on the basis of color or a legacy of oppression and unequal opportunity dating back generations—Obama turns to remedies that are colorblind in application.

> This pattern—of a rising tide lifting minority boats—has certainly held true in the past. The progress made by the previous generations of Latinos and African Americans occurred primarily because the same ladders of opportunity that built the white middle class were for the first time made available to minorities as well.

In this, Obama tells a partial truth. Yes, it was the extension of previously denied opportunities to black and brown folks that allowed minority "boats" to rise, so to speak. But the social movements that forced open those doors of opportunity were hardly race-neutral. Nor did they engage a rhetoric of racial transcendence in advocating for the opening of that opportunity. They were explicitly antiracist movements, which spoke regularly of racism perpetrated by whites in the job and housing markets, schools and elsewhere. And the remedies that helped force open opportunities were not universal—indeed, why would they have been, since whites already had access to them?—but rather, they included measures like affirmative action for hiring, contracting and college admissions. In the realm of both public and private sector employment, race-based affirmative action was critical to opening up professional and managerial ranks to African Americans beginning in the early 1970s.[22]

Ignoring this inconveniently race-conscious aspect of the history about which he was speaking, Obama then suggests that universal efforts like "investments needed to ensure that all children perform at grade level and graduate from high school" and "a plan for universal health care coverage" would do more to eliminate racial disparities and help people of color than race-targeted efforts. Though he offers no reason for why this might be true—no evidence or even analytical support for the claim—he then turns to what in all likelihood is the real motivation for the argument: simple politics. Echoing William Julius Wilson's concerns (and those of Moynihan before him), Obama proclaims, "An emphasis on universal, as opposed to race-specific, programs isn't just good policy; it's also good politics," because of the ability of such efforts, presumably, to gain support across multiple constituencies.[23]

Later, we will explore the reasons why Obama's confidence in universal programs of uplift is largely misplaced. For now, let it suffice to say that the president, for many years, has clearly advocated this approach. Both as a policy advocate, political candidate and now president of the United States, his has been a politics that seeks to downplay the problem of racism and remedy ongoing injustices through race-neutral means.

Not only in his writing, but on the campaign trail as well, Obama evinced a preference for colorblind universalism in public policy and regularly deployed rhetoric suggesting that race and racism were of declining significance to the nation. At an AFL-CIO forum in Las Vegas, for instance, asked how to address persistent health disparities between whites and blacks, candidate Obama pivoted away from the issue, choosing instead to reiterate his support for universal coverage and to discuss the need for blacks to get more exercise and eat healthier foods.[24] Though not blaming the victims in this case—he did, after all, note the way in which poor communities of color often lack access to such foods and rarely have good, safe parks or recreation facilities for local residents to utilize—his comments betrayed a desire to avoid addressing the difficult issues of racial bias in the provision of health care. Likewise, he displayed no interest in commenting on the unique health effects of ongoing racial discrimination, which has been heavily documented by researchers over the past decade. And once again he conflated the subjects of racial disparity and economic disparity, as if to suggest that it is poverty and ghetto life that explain health gaps between whites and blacks. In fact, as we'll see shortly, health outcomes in black America are worse, independent of economic status. Indeed, African Americans with good health care coverage, high incomes and college degrees—not typically to be found in the nation's poorest communities—have health issues that are often worse than those for *poor* whites.

Perhaps there is no clearer evidence of Obama's commitment to colorblind post-racial liberalism than his handling of the Rev. Jeremiah Wright controversy during the presidential campaign. On the one hand, politics alone no doubt dictated that he distance himself from Wright. Once a few of his former pastor's sermons were leaked to the press (and, it should be noted, typically taken horribly out of context in the process), Obama's closeness to

Wright threatened to sink his campaign altogether. Wright's invective against United States foreign policy and the history of racism against peoples of color, combined with what many viewed as the harshness of his tone, was shocking to many white Americans—a group that has rarely been exposed to the raw and prophetic tradition of the black church. That Wright's references to the nation's history were on point (in fact, with regard to U.S. militarism, one could even say he had shown restraint, mentioning only a few examples of American imperialism, while ignoring even stronger case studies) mattered not. For Obama to be linked to a man who had such a dissident view of the inherent goodness of the United States—and acceptance of that goodness, of the exceptionalism of America, is virtually a prerequisite for anyone seeking elected office—was like stepping on a political land mine.

That Obama sought to distance himself from Wright is no surprise, nor, given the political realities with which he was contending, should his desire to do so be seen as especially problematic. It was not *that* he did it, but *how*, that seemed to suggest something deeper than a mere concern for political viability. Indeed, in cutting himself off from Wright, Obama went well beyond what was necessary in order to put himself squarely in the camp of race moderates and post-racial liberals.

His March 18, 2008, speech in Philadelphia, now often referred to as Obama's race speech, or even simply "The Speech,"[25] is considered by some, even only eighteen months later, to be among the greatest political orations in the nation's history. That it was delivered by a man under pressure to clarify his views in the wake of the Wright scandal made it doubly so, in that it became a test of Obama's leadership and ability to rise to the occasion under stress.

Therein, Obama delivered a finely crafted message to the American people, intended to make clear his views on race and its role in shaping the nation. Though he went further than any other presidential candidate in history in candidly speaking about the institutional racism that had long been a formal (and quite legal) reality in the United States, he did so in a way that exemplifies classic post-racial liberalism. During the speech Obama exposed some of the nation's warts, but he eased the embarrassment associated with the process by showering praise upon the United States for its progress and seeking to balance out criticisms of racism with platitudes about black irresponsibility.

First, Obama began by praising the nation's founders as "statesmen and patriots who had traveled across an ocean to escape tyranny and persecution," ignoring for a moment the more literal truth that those who came, while certainly escaping tyranny in the process, did not necessarily come *for* that reason, so much as for land. And of course, their issue wasn't with tyranny in the abstract, which they were all too willing to impose on the indigenous peoples they encountered as well as enslaved Africans (and even the poor and irreligious of their own kind, in the case of the early colonists). It was a necessary platitude perhaps, in that Obama was seeking to become president, and thus could hardly be expected to condemn the Founding Fathers of the nation he was seeking to lead. Yet it also mixed well with the rest of the presentation: a near perfect sampling of post-racial liberal themes and imagery.[26]

When Obama next noted the Founders' decision to allow slavery to continue for the time being as a way to procure the passage of the Constitution—a compromise that many find reprehensible and worthy of moral rebuke, however politically useful it may have been at the time—he quickly parried with praise. After all, as he noted, the "answer to the slavery question was already embedded within the Constitution" because of its promise of *liberty and justice for all.* In other words, the Founders, though flawed, and although they didn't realize they had planted the seeds of slavery's destruction in their final document, must be praised for having done so. That it would actually not be the U.S. Constitution per se, at least in its original form, but rather a well-organized abolitionist movement, several hundred slave rebellions, the John Brown raid at Harper's Ferry, a war that left 600,000 dead, and then hard-fought *amendments* to that Constitution nearly a century later that would ultimately settle the slavery question—at least in writing—seems to escape Obama here. Though Obama went on in the speech to praise those who fought, both in the war and in the civil rights movements, for pushing the nation closer to its vaunted principles, he first made sure to frame his comments with the genius of the white men who set the system up, before praising the real heroes (of color and their white allies) who ultimately brought the formal tyranny of nearly 200 years (and more than 300 going back to the colonial period) to an end.

From there, Obama's colorblind post-racial liberalism kicked into high gear, punctuated by lofty rhetoric about how "we may have different stories, but we hold common hopes," or "we may not look the same and we may not have come from the same place, but we all want to move in the same direction." He then noted how he had won support in "some of the whitest" areas of the country, as evidence that the American people were so hungry "for this message of unity" that they were now willing to get past race and move the country forward by supporting him, a man of color, for president. If whites in South Carolina, where Obama noted "the Confederate flag still flies" (but where, to be sure, he never offered so much as a single significant word of condemnation for that fact) had managed to vote for him in the state primary, then surely the nation must have turned a corner on race, he suggested. That the only whites voting for Obama in the state had been committed Democrats—a distinct minority of the white population—and that the vast majority of whites would vote decisively *against* him in November (an outcome that was utterly predicted and predictable at the time he made this statement) apparently mattered not to Obama and his vision of a post-racial electorate.

Although Obama noted that race had occasionally been an issue in the campaign, he deftly sought to deflect the blame for that fact onto the media, which had "scoured every exit poll" for signs of racism (as if they were looking for a needle in a haystack, or something else equally unlikely to be found), and on occasion deemed him either "too black" or "not black enough." With this trope, Obama sought to place himself in the center of a debate he had wanted no part of, as if to say that anyone who was catching flack from "both sides" must be doing something right. It was Obama's attempt, or so it seemed, to suggest he had been the victim of other peoples' agendas; that he had tried to rise above race politics, only to be forced into discussing the subject by the pernicious machinations of others. Indeed, there was little doubt that he would never have given the race speech at all had it not been for the brewing controversy about a certain pastor from Chicago.

At the point in the speech where Obama turned to the subject of Wright, the Senator criticized him for expressing views that could "widen the racial divide," and which "denigrate the greatness and the goodness of our nation." Though he insisted Wright's words "rightly offend black and white alike," this claim had little resemblance to the truth. Though polls suggested African Americans might have regretted Wright's words, in large measure because of their potential effect on Obama's electoral chances, there is very little to indicate that blacks as a group were offended by them, or even disagreed.

One poll, conducted by FOX News in April 2008, found that whereas the Wright affair had made nearly half of all whites less likely to vote for Barack Obama, only 18 percent of blacks felt the same way. In fact, more blacks said that Obama's closeness to Wright *increased* the likelihood that they would vote for him than said it would decrease their willingness to do so.[27]

Another poll, this time by CBS News and the *New York Times*, discovered that whereas 92 percent of blacks said Wright's statements had no effect on their views of Obama (and only 4 percent said the comments had made them take a dimmer view of the candidate), a full 41 percent of whites indicated that their views of Obama were now more negative because of Wright and, presumably, the senator's connection to him.[28] In effect, Obama's attempt to downplay the racial divide over Wright, by implying that all were "rightly" and similarly offended by him, mirrored his larger attempts to downplay racial divisions more broadly. To admit of the differing perceptions of whites and blacks in this instance, as with any other issue, would be to cast doubt upon the "one America" rhetoric that had by that point become his hallmark.

To reassure whites of his differences with Wright, the candidate insisted that the pastor held a "profoundly distorted view of this country," in that he sees white racism as "endemic," and because he "elevates what is wrong with America above all that we know is right with America." Wright, Obama averred, was being "divisive at a time when we need unity; racially charged at a time when we need to come together to solve a set of monumental problems . . . problems that are neither black or white or Latino or Asian, but rather problems that confront us all." Those problems, according to Obama—and which he insisted were jointly shared—included two wars, terrorism, economic decline, "a chronic health care crisis" and climate change. But not, apparently, insidious discrimination against three of the four groups mentioned by Obama in his litany of unity. To allow that racism were still an issue to be addressed—among the points Jeremiah Wright had been trying to make, after all—would be to allow for a reading of the latter's comments as perhaps quite a bit less incendiary and radical than they had appeared to so many, whose votes Obama now relied upon.

Once having largely dispensed with Rev. Wright, Obama made his one and only real nod to an antiracist narrative, one that recognizes the profound consequences of racism in the life of the nation. Therein he noted, "So many of the disparities that exist in the African American community today can be directly traced to inequalities passed on from an earlier generation that suffered under the brutal legacy of Jim Crow." He even went so far as to mention a part of history about which most are largely unaware, especially most whites, when he mentioned the way that blacks were blocked from housing, including government-backed housing loans via the FHA—an especially important point to make, given the way that this single solitary program had largely created the white middle class in the mid-twentieth century.[29] That Obama was willing to lay blame for the wealth and income disparities between whites and blacks at the feet of institutional bias such as this was meaningful, and among the most honest statements on race ever put forth by a candidate for the U.S. presidency. He followed this up with still more honesty, explaining in quite prosaic detail the way in which so many black folks, especially of Rev. Wright's generation, grew up under crushing conditions of oppression, and that naturally, such experiences would shape their worldviews. Whites, he seemed to be saying, would just have to understand whence the Rev. Wrights of the world were coming.

But then, just as quickly as Obama had tried to contextualize the Reverend's remarks as well as his tone, he again switched gears, noting that anger, the likes of which one can occasionally hear in the black church, is often not productive in that it "distracts attention from solving real problems" and "keeps us from squarely facing our own complicity in our condition." In other words, righteous indignation at systematic injustice distracts black people from the role they themselves are presumed to be playing in their own disempowerment. In effect, Obama seemed to be suggesting that there were co-equal partners in the black condition: past injustice and its legacy on the one hand, but on the other, modern-day black irresponsibility and bad decision making.

Then, as if to further balance out his commentary about the understandable nature of black anger, Obama noted that, "a similar anger exists within segments of the white community." The statement, which seemed to suggest that there was an equivalence between black and white anger, in terms of historic justification, "fudge[d] the difference," as Adam Mansbach puts it, between "institutional racism and white bitterness."[30] In doing so, Obama managed to obscure the nature of structural injustice and to place

personal

black and white anger on the level playing field of mere "feelings," perhaps legitimate, perhaps not, but always merely personal, and never indicative of a deeply ingrained system of oppression deployed against some and in favor of others.

As for that white anger to which Obama was giving voice, it stemmed from unfair accusations of white privilege against those who feel that whatever they have in life, "they've built it from scratch." That he had just finished reciting the institutionalized advantages whites had received, including but not limited to the FHA loan preferences—all of which suggest that however hard whites have worked, they also have had an opportunity structure in place to meet that effort halfway—seemed to matter not a bit. Obama continued in this vein, noting white folks' job insecurities, concerns about cross-town busing for the purpose of integration (which had been all but eliminated by the time of his remarks, and which almost always burdened black children rather than white ones, making this a particularly bizarre reference), and affirmative action.

On this latter subject, Obama was especially craven in pandering to white backlash views, noting the legitimacy of white anger "when they hear that an African American is getting an advantage in landing a good job or a spot in a good college because of an injustice that they themselves never committed." That whites may *hear* that argument made, or even make it themselves, of course, says little about the accuracy of the position. Indeed, Obama well knows that affirmative action has done nothing to displace whites from good jobs or college slots: Whites are still more likely than members of any other racial group to get into their first-choice college,[31] and the vast majority of "good jobs" are held by whites, affirmative action notwithstanding. Nor is it premised on the notion of reparation for past injustice. Rather, and Obama (the former law professor and *Harvard Law Review* editor) surely knows it, affirmative action is predicated on the demonstrably true notion that in the absence of deliberate efforts to recruit, admit, hire, train and promote *qualified* people of color for college slots and professional opportunities, such persons will continue to be overlooked because of racial bias in the *present*. So too, it is premised on the idea that persons of color will continue to be denied full opportunity in the absence of race-conscious efforts at inclusion, thanks to systemic barriers like old boys' networks for jobs and unequal resources in K-12 schooling. In the case of the latter, resource disparities produce students of color who appear less qualified on paper (in terms of past test scores) but who may have every bit as much potential as white students who, given better opportunity, scored higher.[32]

That Obama would obscure the difference between the institutional inequity to which something like affirmative action was directed, and white feelings about those programs, suggests the way that post-racial liberalism often reduces structural forces to interpersonal ones and, in so doing, manages to dumb down our national understanding of how systems operate. As Mansbach puts it, in discussing Obama's race speech:

> To place the experiences of white and black Americans on an equal footing, Obama had to abandon the empirical and speak the language of the emotional. Hence the focus on how people "feel"—privileged or not, racist or not—rather than on the objective realities of what they have and do and say.[33]

Occasionally it seemed as though Obama actually went further than to merely suggest equivalence between the experiences of whites and blacks. Indeed, near the end of his speech, he implied that the responsibility of blacks for solving the racial divide might even be greater than the burden for whites. In discussing what would be necessary on the part of both blacks and whites in order to move the nation "toward a more perfect union," Obama's recommendations appeared strangely non-parallel.

For blacks, he insisted upon the importance of "embracing the burdens" of the past without "becoming victims" of them. Yes, it is necessary to demand justice, he said, but only insofar as the African American community links those demands to the legitimate demands of all Americans for better jobs and health care. That blacks have rarely denied these links seems to escape Obama. Indeed it was the Reverend Jesse Jackson, often perceived as merely a "race hustler" by whites, who went to the white farm belt in his 1984 and 1988 presidential campaigns to explicitly connect the dots between the economic crisis in white communities and black ones.

However, Obama went even further than merely calling for unity on economic justice matters. He then dipped into the well of culture-of-poverty thinking, suggesting that blacks must "take full responsibility for our lives" (implying that blacks, presently, were unwilling to do so), by "spending more time with our children" and "demanding more from our fathers." Given Obama's own abandonment by his father, one can easily understand his personal emphasis on this latter point. Yet it must also be understood that as a memetic device, inserted in a speech on race and racism, it can easily be read by whites as equating the importance of absent fathers and racism in explaining the state of blacks in America today.

From whites, Obama demanded no similar taking of personal responsibility. At no point did he suggest, parallel to his demands for blacks to shape up, that whites must own their own history of biases and prejudices, or the way in which they may have inherited them from their parents or passed them down to their children. To Obama, bad parenting appears to be a trait monopolized by African Americans, and has little to do with the persistent racial biases, which we'll explore more directly in the next chapter, and which seem to be transmitted intergenerationally among whites. Nowhere does he indicate a need for whites to recognize the role that preferential treatment had played in their own lives, even as he had previously acknowledged that preferential treatment, in his discussion of things like the FHA loan program and other discriminatory impediments to equal opportunity. While Obama was comfortable telling black folks to recognize both the institutional and personal contributors to their condition, for whites, the institutional advantages offered over the years were unmentionable, and certainly irremediable. And whereas he insisted that black demands for justice were legitimate, but only to the extent they were linked to the demands of white working people for decent jobs and health care, he offers no symmetrical admonition to the white community, nothing to the effect that white demands for better opportunities must, in order to be legitimate, be linked to black and brown demands for an end to racial discrimination in all arenas of life. No indeed: All he asked of whites was that they "acknowledge" the lived reality of black people, and recognize that discrimination, past and present, is not merely "in the minds of black people," but a real problem to be addressed. Though such a plea may serve as a starting point for dialogue, it asks of whites no real behavioral changes, let alone support for particular policies to address the problem he had just noted was real. Rather, a simple attitude adjustment would presumably suffice.

There was little doubt, of course, that in taking this cautious approach, Obama was carefully reading the pulse of the white public. Indeed, even with his fairly timid articulation of anything that might remotely challenge white thinking, he was criticized mightily from whites on the political right. For instance, and as an indication of how badly many whites in the United States seek to avoid any discussion of white racism, the part of Obama's speech that received the greatest criticism from conservative commentators was the part where he mentioned his white grandmother, and the way that she had occasionally uttered racial or ethnic stereotypes in his presence, or confessed her fear of black men. Though Obama had been trying to point out that we are all complicated—that we are a mixture of better and worse natures, often in conflict, as with the same Reverend Wright he had grown to love, and as with his grandmother, who had sacrificed so much for him—many whites could only take his comment as a slur. And so, former Congressman and current talk show host Joe Scarborough responded to Obama's recitation of his grandmother's biases by blasting the senator for "throwing his grandmother under the bus." Republican advisor Karl Rove likewise employed the "under the bus" imagery in a speech to the Harvard Republicans around the same time, during which he expressly condemned Obama for equating his grandmother's fear of black men with the comments of Reverend Wright.[34] In other words, white people's fears and prejudices towards black men are acceptable, or at least not as offensive to many whites, as Wright's mere recitation of *factual* American history.

In such an atmosphere there is little wonder that candidate Obama would seek to deploy the language of post-racial liberalism—a combination of a rhetoric of racial transcendence and a public policy agenda of colorblind universalism—in order to attract political support for his candidacy. And indeed this tactic may have assisted him in his ability, early on, to garner white votes. Early in his primary run, Obama's white supporters were quite open in their praise for his race-averse approach. So, in a front-page article in the November 10, 2007, edition of the *Wall Street Journal*, white Obama-backers explained that they supported the senator because he makes whites "feel good" about themselves, or because he "doesn't come with the baggage of the civil rights movement."[35] In essence, what at least some of Obama's white supporters seemed to be saying was that his explicit avoidance of race as an issue and his seeming distance from race-based activism was among the principal reasons they were able to support him so intently. While this may suggest the benefits of post-racial liberalism for getting persons of color elected to office, it hardly speaks to the question of whether such an approach is best for addressing persistent inequities, a subject to which we'll turn in the following chapter.[36]

Lest one believe Obama's race-neutral, colorblind approach was merely a matter of political calculation, however, it should be noted that even after he took office, he continued to evince a similar approach to matters of race as the one he had put forth before the November 2008 election. So at the press conference marking the one-hundredth day of his administration, he was asked how he would seek to address the impacts of the economic downturn on black men. It is worth recounting the entire exchange, in order to fully appreciate how averse the president is to addressing racial inequity directly. To wit, the following interaction between Andre Showell, of Black Entertainment Television (BET), and President Obama on April 29, 2009:

> SHOWELL: As the entire nation tries to climb out of this deep recession, in communities of color the circumstances are far worse. The black unemployment rate, as you know, is in the double digits, and in New York City, for example, the black unemployment rate for men is near 50 percent. My question tonight is, given this unique and desperate circumstance, what specific policies can you point to that will target these communities?
>
> PRESIDENT OBAMA: Well, keep in mind that every step we're taking is designed to help all people. But folks who are most vulnerable are most likely to be helped because they need the most help. So when we passed the Recovery Act, for example, and we put in place provisions that would extend unemployment insurance or allow you to keep your health insurance even if you've lost your job, that probably disproportionately impacted those communities that had lost their jobs. . . . So my general approach is that if the economy is strong, that will lift all boats—as long as it is also supported by, for example, strategies around college affordability, and job training, tax cuts for working families as opposed to the wealthiest, that level the playing field and ensure bottom-up economic growth. And I'm confident that that will help the African American community live out the

American Dream, at the same time that it's helping communities all across the country.[37]

Even when served up a rather safe question, to which he might have responded by indicating a willingness to specifically address the depression-level economics of black America (even while reiterating his support for universal policies as well), Obama punted, apparently content to address such racial inequity through universal policy options alone.

President Obama further reiterated his colorblind approach in the waning days of 2009, after being pressed by the Congressional Black Caucus to focus some attention on the unique economic challenges facing the African American community. In response to the CBC's critique, Obama replied that he "cannot pass laws that say 'I'm just helping black folks.' I'm the president of the entire United States," and that instead, his goal is to pass laws "that help all people, particularly those who are most vulnerable and most in need. . . . That in turn is going to help lift up the African American community."[38]

Of course, it is worth noting that the Congressional Black Caucus had not called for Obama to push for programs aimed only at helping black people. Rather, its members had requested that he speak to the specific concerns of African Americans, who were being especially battered by the economic downturn, and to include some specific policy proposals to address those unique burdens, within the context of a larger universal effort. Yet Obama, as has long been his practice, presents universalism as if it cannot exist side by side with race-specific efforts at uplift. To the President and others who embrace colorblind post-racial liberalism,

universal efforts must be an alternative to race-specificity, replacing the latter with the bland ecumenism of the former, irrespective of the specific obstacles still faced by persons of color on the basis of race alone.

Tellingly, however, the dodge hasn't worked, at least not for those right-wing commentators insistent on making Obama over as a race radical, despite all evidence to the contrary. Prominent conservatives have claimed that even universal programs, because they would disproportionately help blacks (because blacks are more likely to be uninsured, unemployed, poor, etc.), are really nothing more than a form of stealth reparations for slavery.[39] Talk show host Glenn Beck, for instance, has jumped on Obama's mention during the campaign (and since) that blacks would disproportionately benefit from universal health care coverage—if simply because they were disproportionately sick and uninsured—by insisting that such comments prove the president's real motivation for health care reform isn't health at all, but rather obtaining reparations.[40] Obama is using health care reform to "settle old racial scores," according to Beck. Putting aside the fundamental illogic of believing health care to be reparations—after all, what kind of reparations requires its beneficiaries to get sick first in order to get paid?—the political implications of Beck's screed should be noted here, as we move into the next chapter.

Clearly, if even colorblind, race-neutral and universal rhetoric and policy pronouncements are likely to be recast by the right as racially-specific and race-motivated, it becomes an open question as to whether the politics of post-racial liberalism can succeed, even on its own terms. If post-racial liberalism presumes that its primary strength is political viability, and yet those who practice it continue to be pilloried as agents of racial score-settling and reverse discrimination anyway, one has to wonder just how viable the approach truly is in practice. And given the potential downsides of the post-racial narrative and colorblind universalism (when pushed to the exclusion of any race-specific policy directives), it may be that all post-racial liberalism accomplishes is to take antiracism off the table, while leaving racism—in both its institutional and interpersonal forms—dangerously in place.

Some, of course, suggest that President Obama is simply biding his time, that eventually, perhaps in a second term, he will tackle racism and discrimination and a host of other issues, when doing so would have less political risk associated with the move. But this kind of thinking is fraught with dangers. To begin, he is not guaranteed a second term. In fact, his timidity could put such a damper on the voter turnout of his base—especially in off-year and mid-term elections—that he loses the working majority in Congress that he would need in order to accomplish anything remotely progressive, assuming for the moment that he were even inclined to head in such a direction. This is precisely what happened in 1994, for instance, after Bill Clinton's timidity around health care left his voter base deflated, and the right emboldened.

Additionally, if the president, having staked out his ground in the camp of post-racial liberalism and colorblind universalism, were to eventually decide to raise the issue of racism and discrimination, he would violate the new "norm of silence" about race that he had helped create. The backlash this would engender, from political opponents and even many allies, could potentially result in major losses in the rest of his public policy agenda, making it unlikely that he would risk it. To act as though race were no longer really an issue, only to then announce, say, six years into one's presidency that you had been, in effect, just kidding, would be seen as a cynical political move and would not likely endear Obama to lawmakers, even in the Democratic Party. It is also the kind of blatantly manipulative shift in position that Obama has studiously tried *not* to evince over the years. It would be almost entirely out of character.

If President Obama has, for several years now, articulated his faith in colorblind universalism and has employed a rhetoric of racial transcendence, the most likely conclusion to be drawn from such a thing is that he really believes in them, and that he means what he says. To assume otherwise is to place considerable faith in the intentionality of one man to somehow shift gears and "do the right thing," even though there is no evidence of him having done this at any point, ever, in his career previously. It is a fundamentally dangerous and illiberal notion in which to place much faith.

TWO

The Trouble with Post-racial Liberalism

"Whether race is a burden or a benefit is all the same to the race-neutral theorists; that is what they mean when they speak of being colorblind. They are colorblind, all right—blind to the consequences of being the wrong color in America today."

—Julian Bond, Chairman, NAACP, 2003[41]

Post-racial liberalism, characterized by its rhetoric of racial transcendence and its public policy agenda of colorblind universalism, bases its claims for legitimacy on two pillars of presumed truth. The first is a presumption of racism's declining significance, to conjure William Julius Wilson's terminology. This argument holds that much, perhaps even most of the inequality between whites and people of color—especially blacks—in the United States, is no longer caused by racism and race-based discrimination. Rather, economic forces, and even ingrained cultural factors within the African American community have overtaken the role of racism in explaining the conditions of life faced by black and brown folks, especially the urban poor. The second presumption of post-racial liberalism and its proponents is that whether or not this first maxim is true—and they militantly insist that it is—we must act as though it were, for the political reality is such that whites simply will not support, in any real measure, policies that seek to target opportunity specifically to people of color or address racial inequities directly. That these two positions are internally inconsistent, as noted previously—in that the first presumes white folks are now committed to racial equity, while the second presumes they are not—matters little, it seems, to the apostles of colorblindness.

But is either presumption of post-racial liberalism accurate? Is colorblind universalism sufficient to ameliorate persistent racial inequities in income, wealth, housing, education and health care? Is a rhetoric of racial transcendence necessary in order to build political support for progressive politics in the modern era? And what are the consequences of this approach, not only for the political arena, but for our private lives as well? What would be the impact of colorblindness as a paradigm for thought and action among employers, teachers and others who interact with a racially diverse public? Would such an approach lessen racial discrimination or potentially make it worse?

THE REALITY OF RACIAL DISPARITIES

Before we can answer these questions, a bit of preliminary groundwork is in order. After all, although both the proponents of post-racial liberalism and those who put forth traditional antiracist theories agree that there are significant racial disparities that must be addressed—albeit through different means—it is not the case that everyone recognizes the depths of those inequities. Many readers may be unfamiliar with the evidence in this regard, and so a brief review may be helpful to frame the discussion to follow.

Sadly, presumptions of post-raciality are not new. In fact, such presumptions have long been the norm, especially among whites, for whom an understanding of ingrained racial inequities has long been absent. So, for instance, even in the 1960s, at a time when all would now agree the United States was a profoundly unequal place, where racial discrimination was deeply systematized, most whites saw little about which to be concerned. According to Gallup polls taken in 1962 and 1963, between two-thirds and nearly 90 percent of whites said that blacks were treated equally with regard to jobs, schooling and housing opportunities.[42] That most whites could believe such a thing, even at the height of the civil rights movement—which, by definition, was animated by the reality that treatment was far from equal—says much about the pathological nature of white denial. Indeed, in 1963, three-fourths of whites said the civil rights movement was pushing too fast for change, and asking for "too much."[43] This, during a year in which blacks were being hosed down in the streets of Birmingham by racist police, and blown up at the 16th Street Baptist Church there, as well as a year in which Mississippi NAACP chair Medgar Evers was murdered in his driveway, and Alabama Governor George Wallace promised to maintain segregation forever.

But putting aside the extent to which whites perceive opportunity to be equal—and thus, the extent to which bigotry and discrimination against people of color continue to be real problems—the sad truth is that most whites fail to possess even the slightest awareness that people of color face any different life situations at all, regardless of cause. Recent polling has found that most whites believe blacks are just as well off as they are when it comes to jobs and income.[44] This, despite the fact that African Americans are twice as likely as whites to be employed in low-wage jobs and twice as likely to be unemployed, in good times or bad.[45] As of 2009, even black men with college degrees were nearly twice as likely to be unemployed as their white counterparts.[46] Overall, according to the most recent data available at the time of this writing, blacks with bachelor's degrees are twice as likely to be unemployed as non-Hispanic whites; Latinos with at least a college degree are nearly two-thirds more likely than non-Hispanic whites to be unemployed, and Asians with at least a college degree are about 13 percent more likely to be out of work than similar whites.[47] What's more, the earnings gap between college-educated whites and blacks has actually grown in recent years, thanks to the tendency for persons of color to be let go first during economic downturns, in part because they obtained their positions later than whites, who were in the pipeline for the best jobs far earlier.[48] In other words, the notion that all workers are in the same boat, or that the disadvantages experienced by African Americans and other people of color are merely caused by poverty status or other human capital factors like education, is clearly false.

On average, blacks are about three times more likely than non-Hispanic whites to be poor and three and a half times as likely to be extremely poor.[49] Spells of unemployment also last longer for people of color. So, for instance, as of August 2009, out-of-work black men remain unemployed for about seven more weeks than white men, and unemployed black women remain out of work for about five more weeks than white women, on average. Asian men and women also face longer spells of unemployment, compared to whites: about seven weeks and four weeks more time out of work than their white counterparts, respectively.[50] It should be noted that to be counted in unemployment data, an individual must be actively seeking employment, so this data represents the difference between whites and folks of color who are all actively seeking jobs. It is not, as some believe, due to persons of color having less attachment to the labor market, possessing different work ethics, or merely not looking hard enough for employment.

Beyond mere unemployment, there are substantial gaps in terms of what kinds of jobs even the employed have, with many of these gaps playing out racially. So, for instance, whites continue to dominate the top jobs in America, holding approximately 83 percent of all management-level positions. Considering that this number includes public sector management positions as well (such as positions in schools, government, etc.), in which people of color are somewhat better represented than in the economy as a whole, it is safe to say that whites hold more than 85 percent of such jobs in the private and higher-paying sector.[51] And yet whites are only about 68 percent of the national population. During the recent economic downturn, the gaps between whites and persons of color—both black and Latino—have actually grown at the upper end of the employment spectrum, with whites capturing a higher percentage of upper-income jobs and persons of color a lower percentage, than at any time in the past decade.[52] Even Chinese-American professionals, who are on balance a highly educated group—and thus should be expected to earn relatively high incomes when compared to whites—earn only about 56 percent of what white professionals earn, despite their equal or greater educational credentials.[53]

That most whites are unaware of these and other facts that collectively demonstrate the reality of racial inequity in America, is indisputable. According to the results of one national survey, 70 percent of whites demonstrate at least one if not several erroneous beliefs about the well-being of persons of color relative to whites,[54] presuming a far greater degree of equity between the groups than exists in practice. A Kaiser Family Foundation report from several years ago indicated significant ignorance about matters of basic health and well-being, and the disparities between whites and blacks in that regard. According to Kaiser, two-thirds of whites think blacks are every bit as well off as whites when it comes to getting routine medical care when they need it.[55] In truth, African Americans are far more likely than whites to lack health insurance coverage, and thus have a much harder time accessing routine and quality care.[56]

The most telling evidence of racial inequity, however, is to be found in data on relative net worth and assets. While incomes between similarly educated whites and persons of color have narrowed somewhat in the past two decades—though still, whites at every age level and educational attainment level continue to earn, on average, about 20 percent more than their black counterparts—gaps in wealth are truly stunning and have tended to grow over time, rather than narrow. At the beginning of the decade of the 2000s, for example, the median net worth for white households was approximately eleven times the median net worth for black households and eight times the median net worth for Latino households.[57] The typical young black couple, though earning about the same as their white counterparts (assuming they have comparable educations), will start out with a net worth less than one-fifth that of the typical young white couple: a difference of over $20,000.[58]

Even that level of division masks a deeper and more disturbing reality, however. For blacks and Latinos, most wealth and assets are bound up with home value. For whites, home value represents only about 30 percent of overall wealth, as they are far more likely to possess financial instruments such as stocks, commercial real estate and other more easily liquidated and accessible assets. Indeed, once home equity is excluded from consideration, median white household wealth is nearly twenty times the median for black households and twelve times the median for Latinos. If the average white family were black, their net worth would be at least $100,000 less than it currently is.[59]

These gaps manifest at every income level, and do not merely reflect the extremes of white wealth and black and brown poverty. So, for instance, the poorest whites in terms of income (those in the bottom fifth of all households) still possess, on average, about $24,000 in assets, largely because they may have a small piece of property passed on to them from other family members. But blacks in the poorest fifth of all households possess, on average, only $57 in assets, for a white-to-black wealth ratio at this level of 421:1. These poorest whites also have forty-eight times the wealth of the poorest Latinos. In the middle fifth of income earners, white households have 5.2 times the wealth, on average, of the typical black household in the middle class, and 5.3 times

assets

that of middle-class Latinos. In the upper-income bracket, among households with incomes that place them in the top fifth of all income earners, whites have 3.2 times more wealth, on average, than comparable blacks, and nearly three times more than the typical Latino household.[60]

As a result of these disparities, black families are far more vulnerable than their white counterparts to economic downturns, in that they do not have reserve assets on hand with which to pad their economic situation in case of a layoff. More than half of all black families are so asset-poor that they could not sustain as many as three months without income and still remain above the poverty line, while only one in four white families are equally asset-poor.[61]

RACE-BASED INJURY, INHERITED DISADVANTAGE AND ONGOING DISCRIMINATION

It is one thing, however, to acknowledge persistent gaps in well-being between whites and people of color, and quite another to understand the causes for those disparities. The proponents of color-blind liberalism seek to explain most of the racial gaps today by way of factors other than racism and discrimination. Though they certainly do not deny the weight of past oppression, these theorists tend to minimize the extent to which past injustice determines the current status of blacks and other people of color in the United States. Rather, they claim to find the source of much inequity in race-neutral macroeconomic developments, such as the decline of manufacturing employment and a shift to service-sector jobs—which, according to Wilson, has created a spatial mismatch between where black people live and where most of those new jobs are—and additionally in certain attributes, behavioral and cultural, which they see manifested in urban spaces and which they believe keep people of color down, relative to whites.

Yet a careful examination of both the weight of past racial injustice and current evidence of ongoing racial bias and discrimination, calls into question the veracity of the post-racial narrative. Acts of race-specific domination and injustice, both historically and today, exact a much greater toll on black and brown communities than the post-racial liberals—and needless to say conservatives—are prepared to admit. As such, the rhetoric of racial transcendence is dishonest, in that it obscures the power of racism and its impact on present-day communities of color, and its advocacy of colorblind universalism at the level of public policy is destined to fail. After all, it is impossible to solve a problem if the source of that problem is ignored. Even if universal programs of uplift for all in need—in terms of jobs, schools and health care—were valuable (and surely they are), they cannot close racial gaps in income, wealth or health so long as those gaps are being replicated by way of racism and discrimination.

Recognizing the Weight of the Past

While a full recitation of how existing inequities carry over from past race-based oppression would fill volumes, a brief mention of some of the highlights of that oppression is in order, so that we can fully appreciate the cornerstone elements of institutional racial division in the United States.

On the one hand, blacks were subjected to a vicious history of enslavement by whites, under which as much as a trillion dollars in unpaid labor was provided to whites, and for the benefit of the national economy.[62] Furthermore, indigenous persons suffered the theft of their land and violent conquest (as did those residing in Northern Mexico when their land was annexed to the United States). Blacks, Latinos and Chinese workers suffered forced labor (the latter especially as workers on the transcontinental railroad), and all non-whites experienced either *de jure* or *de facto* segregation from the late 1800s until the 1960s.

Racism manifested not only in violent terrorist attacks against communities of color (as with thousands of lynchings, bombings, and acts of arson, or the dozens of white-led race riots against communities of color during the early to mid 1900s),[63] but also in more institutionalized processes. For instance, for many years, persons of color were blocked from access to the skilled trades, and union bosses and politicians alike colluded to allow for the ongoing segregation of labor.[64] Politicians further sedimented inequality by institutionalizing racial discrimination in the awarding of GI Bill benefits, by allowing states to set their own eligibility standards. Such a practice gave Southern states the green light to deny benefits to blacks or to ensure that, even if benefits were awarded, black recipients who had served the country in combat would yet be relegated to the worst jobs and barred from mostly white colleges.[65] Even in states outside the South, blacks faced obstacles to their ability to fully utilize GI Bill benefits, with black workers in places like the San Francisco Bay Area facing regular relegation to the lowest-wage jobs available, despite their military service.[66] Nationally, only 4 percent of college students enrolled under the GI Bill following World War II were African American, in large measure because of ongoing barriers to full access.[67] Likewise, blacks were largely blocked from participating in most of the New Deal programs so vital to economic recovery after the Great Depression. Indeed, until Social Security policies were changed in the 1950s, two decades after the program's creation, about three in four blacks were barred from participation, by way of exclusions implemented in the law that applied to domestic workers and agricultural labor (which comprised the bulk of black employment nationally).[68] As a result of their exclusion from retirement programs, African Americans were forced to continue working well into their seventies, far more often than comparable whites, who had been provided with a safety net in their old age.

Blacks were also provided with very limited educational opportunities throughout this period. In the South, spending for black schools was only about one-third of the amount spent for white schools, per capita, and by 1930, one-third of Southern counties had no four-year high schools for black students at all.[69] Schools attended by blacks were far more crowded, had far fewer resources and were largely removed from the broader opportunity structures used by whites to pass down advantages intergenerationally. That public schooling was separate and profoundly unequal is an understatement of rather dramatic proportions.

The very government that was actively suppressing opportunity for persons of color was directly creating it for whites, however. From the Naturalization Act of 1790, which recognized whiteness and citizenship as synonymous and exclusively so for nearly a century, to fugitive slave laws that favored white property rights over the human rights of African Americans, white preference and privilege was normalized from the nation's beginning. Indeed, it had been so dating back to colonial times, when European indentured servitude had been abolished in favor of chattel enslavement for blacks. In the mid to late 1800s, even as enslavement was coming to an end, and promises of equity began to flow from the lips of national leaders, the state moved to enshrine huge preferences for whites. So, for example, the Homestead Act, passed in 1862, ultimately distributed nearly 250 million acres of land to 1.5 million homesteading families, virtually all of them white. Today, at least 20 million white Americans continue to benefit from those early land giveaways, either by virtue of still holding said property in the possession of their families, or by having been able to sell the land and reap the benefits of those sales intergenerationally.[70] Other estimates place the number of living Homestead Act descendants at closer to *50 million*, with almost none of these being persons of color.[71]

Then, as mentioned previously, the creation of the Federal Housing Administration home loan program—which guaranteed mortgages written by banks to working-class families who otherwise would have been locked out of the housing market—subsidized white wealth creation in the mid 1900s, even as people of color were facing intense housing discrimination. As many as one-third of all mortgages written in the post–World War II period were written under the FHA and VA loan programs, amounting to approximately $120 billion in housing equity, almost exclusively for whites. These mortgages represented approximately half of all suburban housing in America at mid-century. By 1962, 40 percent of all white mortgages were being paid through the preferential lending policies of the FHA or Veteran's Administration programs to which most all people of color were being denied access.[72] Combined with the GI Bill, which placed the lion's share of nearly $100 billion worth of benefits in the hands of white veterans, these efforts can safely be credited with the creation of the white middle class.[73]

The impact of this institutionalized discrimination and white racial preference has been profound, and it is mightily implicated in the current maldistribution of resources between whites and persons of color. Returning now to the issue of racial wealth gaps, there is no question that much of that gap reflects the generations of unequal opportunity that allowed the enrichment of whites at the expense of individuals and communities of color. The best predictor of a young family's net worth, after all, is the net worth of their parents,[74] as up to 80 percent of family wealth derives from intergenerational transfers of assets between parents and children.[75] Some of this transfer occurs upon parental death, but much of it transpires while the parents are still alive, as with down-payment assistance for a home or assistance with college tuition. And when it comes to the net worth of the parents of today's youth—themselves mostly members of the baby-boom generation—the advantages for whites and disadvantages experienced by folks of color are extreme.

Young whites today are about twice as likely as young blacks to find themselves in families where their parents are in a position to help them financially.[76] Because of past inequity of opportunity, white families were able to accumulate assets and pass them down to their children, while black families have not had the same ability. Whereas one in four white families have received an inheritance sufficient to put a down payment on a house, only 3.5

percent of black families have: a ratio of approximately 7:1. Not only are whites more likely to receive some form of intergenerational bequest, the average value of those handed-down benefits is 3.5 times greater than the value of benefits received by blacks from their families.[77]

One of the principal forms of assistance provided by white families to their children (and in large part because past advantages have put them in a position to do so) is with college tuition assistance. The families of black students are only one-third as likely as white families to be able to pay the entire cost of their child's education, and on average, black students' families are only able to cover about 42 percent of the cost of college at the nation's most highly rated (and expensive) schools, while white families are able to cover, on average, roughly 74 percent of the total cost.[78] And contrary to popular belief, black college students do not reap a disproportionate amount of financial aid or scholarships to make up the difference. Scholarships targeted specifically to people of color represent only one-quarter of one percent (0.25 percent) of all scholarship dollars,[79] and only about 3.5 percent of students of color receive any kind of race-based scholarship for college.[80] The different abilities of white and black families to pay the cost of higher education for their children no doubt helps explain why the median debt for blacks who go on to receive their PhDs is roughly double the median debt for similar whites: about $39,000, compared to nearly $21,000.[81]

To pay for a child's college education—which whites are in a position to do far more readily, thanks to a history of unequal opportunity—has a huge snowball effect. First, it reduces the debt load carried by young whites at the outset of their careers. This then improves their credit rating and lowers their debt-to-income ratio, thereby improving the odds of being able to buy a home and begin to accumulate one's own assets at an early age. It is in this way that the inertia of past inequity carries over into present and future generations.

Acknowledging Racial Bias in the Present—The Persistence of Prejudice

Unfortunately, it is not just the weight of the past that explains persistent racial gaps in wealth, health and occupational status. Though commentators are quick to pronounce racial prejudices all but dead—especially in the so-called age of Obama—the evidence suggests a deep-seated and negative color-consciousness among large numbers of white Americans.[82] This negative color-consciousness manifests both at the level of personal bias, or prejudice, and with institutional mistreatment, in the form of discrimination. That large numbers of whites continue to view people of color through lenses that are clouded by bias suggests that the rhetoric of racial transcendence is asking us to embrace a fictional narrative. Post-racial liberalism, by pronouncing an age of racial ecumenism and harmony, finesses the truth about this bias, thereby making it harder to address.

First, and before examining discriminatory treatment, let us examine the research on personal bias. The evidence in this regard is all too clear: Notwithstanding protestations to the contrary, ongoing racial bias is all too common among large numbers of white Americans. Although most whites have internalized the sense that overt expressions of racial hostility are inappropriate in mixed company, even blatantly hostile remarks and comments are quite frequent in all-white settings.[83] Disturbingly, even those whites who engage in positive and warm interactions with people of color on a fairly regular basis will often fall into these forms of verbal denigration when amongst themselves. One study, involving 626 white students at more than two dozen colleges, found that when asked to keep journals documenting any racially insensitive or racist comments, jokes, incidents or actions on the part of their white friends, participants in the study were able to document more than 7,500 blatantly racist events or incidents in a six-to-ten-week period, or roughly a dozen instances each week witnessed by each white person in the study.[84] Multiplied by millions of whites in colleges, or more broadly, by 200 million whites nationwide, one begins to see the possible magnitude of even blatant white racism in the early twenty-first century.

According to readily available survey data, about six in ten whites are willing to *admit* to believing at least one racist stereotype about blacks to be true: from a belief that blacks are generally less intelligent to beliefs that blacks are naturally more aggressive, lazier, and would rather live on welfare than work for a living.[85] Many of these studies have found that while whites are typically adamant about not being racist, those same whites, once pushed to dig more deeply into their perspectives, often cut loose with any number of anti-black views, such as the notion that "blacks lack a strong work ethic," or that blacks are "less responsible" than whites.[86] Although many whites refuse to admit that they harbor racial prejudices, there is often a substantial difference between stated beliefs and deeper opinion. For instance, one study of whites at three selective universities found that when asked a simple question about their support for, or opposition to, interracial marriage, 80 percent expressed support. But once subjected to the in-depth interviews, less than half of those who claimed to be supportive of such unions stuck with that position, while the rest modified their support substantially, revealing in the process significant reservations they continued to have about interracial relationships.[87]

Whites in metropolitan areas are significantly more likely to hold racist views, with more than half (and often as many as three-quarters) believing that blacks are generally lazier than whites, less intelligent than whites and more likely to prefer welfare to work. At least one in five whites in metropolitan areas hold racist views across the spectrum of categories, and could reasonably be considered severely racist in outlook.[88]

White racism is so entrenched, in fact, that as many as one in four whites says the ideal neighborhood would have *no blacks at all*. While some may seek to chalk up such answers to class bias rather than racial animus (or perhaps a more benign tendency to prefer living around people with whom you share a common cultural background), research has found that anti-black stereotypes are four times more important than mere in-group preferences, and *seven times* more important than class-based prejudices in explaining why these whites prefer black-free neighborhoods.[89] Significantly, white biases against the presence of blacks in their neighborhoods are *not*, at least in the collective sense, the result of having had personal negative experiences such as rising crime rates or declining property values, as is often claimed. Research has found, for instance, that whites began to flee public schools in metropolitan areas long before busing, and long before they could have claimed any decline in the quality of their formerly white-majority schools. So, for instance, in Washington, D.C., St. Louis, Philadelphia, Chicago and Baltimore, formerly white public schools were already on the way to being majority black by the early 1960s.[90] In Matteson, Illinois, an area outside of Chicago, white residents began to flee in the early 1980s as African Americans began to move to the community. From 1980 to 1997 the percentage of Matteson residents who were white declined by half, and by 2002, only a third of the town's residents were white. Although whites who left the community insist they did so because of rising crime and declining property values, during the period of racial transition crime actually held steady or declined, housing prices rose and the median income in the increasingly black community *grew* by 73 percent.[91]

In part, white biases against people of color stem from media coverage that over-represents blacks in pathological and deviant roles, from criminals to the long-term welfare–dependent underclass.[92] Indeed, research from scholars at the University of Illinois has found that the more news one watches—be it local or from the national networks—the more likely one is to negatively stereotype blacks when it comes to aggressiveness and impoverishment. According to the research, the effect of news viewing on racist attitudes is independent of pre-existing racial views, gender, age, race, education levels, political ideology, income, levels of neighborhood diversity and even the crime rate in the viewer's own community. In fact, as much as one-fourth of all stereotypical belief about blacks can be explained *solely* by levels of news viewing, independent of these other factors.[93] No doubt media exposure can help explain why 95 percent of whites say they picture a black person when asked to envision a typical drug user,[94] even though the data indicates that blacks are only about 13 or 14 percent of users, while non-Hispanic whites represent the clear majority—typically over 70 percent—of all drug users.[95]

Not all racial bias is blatant however. Indeed, much of the research in recent years indicating the persistence of white racial biases has been in the area of implicit, often subconscious prejudice, which, however subtle, can still contribute to unequal treatment of people of color in given situations. Implicit Association Tests (IATs), which have been administered to hundreds of thousands of people in recent years, indicate that the vast majority of whites hold implicit biases in favor of whites and against African Americans. The group Americans for American Values provides an easy-to-understand description of how implicit association tests work:

> The IAT uses reaction time measurement to look at subconscious bias. To take a simple example, imagine that you are asked to associate a list of positive words (pretty, sweet, calm) with a list of flower names. Next, you are asked to associate a list of negative words (ugly, scary, freaky) with a list of insect names. So far, so easy, right? Most of us like flowers and aren't crazy about bugs. But what if you reverse it? You are in front of a computer screen and the left half of the screen contains a picture of a spiny poisonous caterpillar and the word "calm," while on the right hand of the screen is a picture of a tulip and the word "freaky." When a positive word *or* an insect name comes up, you press the left arrow. When a negative word or a flower name comes up, you press the right arrow. The second task turns out to be complicated—we don't generally associate insects with positive words. This com-

> plication leads us to do worse (react more slowly) on a test that pairs insects with "pretty," "sweet" and "calm" than one that pairs insects with "ugly," "scary" and freaky." By measuring reaction times in tests like these . . . scientists are able to measure your association of positive words with flowers and negative words with insects. We call the positive association a preference and the negative association a bias.[96]

When administered to test for racial biases, the IATs flash racially identifiable faces on the screen, paired with either positive sounding or negative sounding words, and then compare how quickly associations are made between white or black faces, for instance, and certain words, either positive or negative.[97] According to the research:

> When given a test of unconscious stereotyping, nearly ninety percent of whites who have taken the test implicitly associate the faces of black Americans with negative words and traits such as evil character or failure. That is, they have more trouble linking black faces to pleasant words and positive features than they do for white faces. . . . In addition, when whites are shown photos of black faces, even for only thirty milliseconds, key areas of their brains that are designed to respond to perceived threats light up automatically.[98]

Interestingly, implicit bias in favor of one's own group and against others does not appear to be the result of natural in-group/out-group bonding and categorizing. Rather, the results from hundreds of thousands of IATs that have been administered suggest that they stem from fairly intense social conditioning. Thus, whites, Latinos and Asians all show similar levels of pro-white and anti-black biases, and blacks, far from demonstrating significant pro-black and anti-white bias, are roughly split between those who have implicit pro-black bias, no apparent bias whatsoever and even implicit *pro-white bias*.[99]

These studies have found a clear divide between the claims people make about their own biases and the reality of their internalized stereotypes. So, for instance, one study of more than 45,000 people sought to explore the extent to which respondents held implicit biases against indigenous people in the United States. Although most claimed outwardly that they perceived Native Americans as actually being "more American" than whites, IATs discovered that these same individuals most often associated white faces with the concept of being "American," and were far more likely to do so than to view Native American faces that way.[100]

Other research has found a similar split between the non-racist persona that people carry around with them publicly, and the private biases they continue to hold inside. In one classic experiment, a black actor and a white actor engaged in an argument. On the tape shown to one group of whites, the black actor shoves the white actor out of the way. On the tape shown to a second group, it is the white actor who does the shoving. In all other respects the tapes were the same (and the whites viewing the different films had been randomly selected, so they too were functionally no different). Afterward, the white respondents were asked a series of questions about what they had seen. Among them was a question that asked whether they perceived the shove administered at the end of the argument as aggressive or violent. Three out of four whites who had seen the black actor do the shoving answered yes. But only 17 percent of the whites who had seen the white actor administer the exact same kind of shove felt the act had been aggressive or violent.[101] Although this study was conducted in the 1970s, there is little reason to believe that time alone would change the way white Americans, at a subconscious level, perceive aggression in blacks as opposed to other whites.

More important, additional studies since that time have found similar results: One found that even as children, whites view blacks as more aggressive than other whites engaged in the very same behavior,[102] and another found that white preschoolers, when looking at pictures of faces that are racially ambiguous and expressing anger, are more likely to classify those faces as black, whereas there is no tendency to over-classify racially ambiguous faces as black when they are smiling.[103]

More recently, in "shoot or hold fire" simulations, in which blacks and whites are shown engaged in a variety of ambiguous activities, participants are quicker to shoot unarmed blacks and to hold fire on whites, even when the latter *are* armed and dangerous.[104] These tendencies, it should be noted, bear no relationship to the degree of overt racial bias expressed by participants in pre-interviews. Rather, they seem tied to implicit, even subconscious biases, which research shows can be easily triggered in situations where common stereotypes of racial groups are made salient.

Even more disturbing, studies have found that whites often fabricate memories of events in ways that fit common racial stereotypes. For instance, in one study, participants were given details of an assault case as if they were in the role of jurors. Asked to remember the case details later, participants overwhelmingly *misremembered* aggressive conduct by blacks in the stories, even when such conduct did not occur, and they were far less likely to remember aggressive conduct by whites, even when, in the narratives given to them, it *did* occur.[105]

In another case, participants were shown news stories about crime in which the color of the shown perpetrator was digitally manipulated. By large margins, respondents were more likely to remember the race of the perpetrator when he was black, and often even misremembered the perpetrator as black when he was not.[106] In one particular study, even when the person committing a crime was not shown and his race was not mentioned in the newscast, 42 percent of participants in the study remembered seeing a perpetrator, and of these, two-thirds "remembered" the offender as black.[107] An additional study found that when shown mug shots of blacks, as opposed to whites, respondents were far more likely to presume guilt, even when the available facts in evidence were the same.[108]

Here it is worth quoting Linda Hamilton Krieger and Susan Fiske, from their 2006 *California Law Review* article on implicit bias:

> As social psychologists John Bargh and James Uleman, among others, have demonstrated, merely encountering a member of a stereotyped group primes the trait constructs associated with, and in a sense, constituting the stereotype. Once activated, these constructs can function as implicit expectancies, spontaneously shaping the perceiver's perception, characterization, memory and judgment of the stereotyped target.[109]

Disturbingly, advocates of post-racial liberalism ignore or finesse evidence of implicit racial bias, preferring to minimize its importance. Yet, in their denials and dismissals, post-racial liberals say more about their own intellectual dishonesty than they say about the social science in question. To wit, Stanford law professor Richard Thompson Ford, who dismisses the implicit bias research, noting that one of its creators insists the research says nothing about the intent of persons to discriminate and should not be used to suggest otherwise.[110] But of course, no one claims the IAT says anything about conscious racist intent. After all, the entire basis of the research is to explore how bias can manifest *without* conscious intent. That is the entire point, as Ford must surely know. But the fact that much bias is unintentional does not alter the reality that it has the potential to exact real damage.

More Than Just Prejudice: Racial Discrimination in the New Millennium

Of course, the mere fact of implicit (or even explicit) racial bias as a persistent problem within white America does not, in and of itself, suggest the extent to which racial discrimination—actual mistreatment of people of color—is likely to manifest. Some may contend that although prejudice is still with us, the ability of whites to act on that prejudice has been mightily constrained by legal prohibitions against discrimination, and perhaps the increasing social unacceptability of racism and race-based mistreatment since the 1960s. Apparently this is the view of white Americans, by and large. To wit, white responses to an early 2009 ABC News/*Washington Post* poll, in which 83 percent insisted blacks have just as good a chance as whites to get a job for which they're qualified, and 81 percent said they believe blacks receive equal treatment in housing.[111]

Yet these post-racial hopes are ill conceived. Evidence of racial discrimination in employment, housing, education and health care, not to mention the criminal justice system, abounds. That advocates of post-racial liberalism so often ignore that evidence says nothing about its persuasiveness.

Racism, Discrimination and Employment

Contributing to the aforementioned employment, income and wealth gaps between whites and people of color is an ongoing pattern of race-based discrimination in the job market. So, for instance, a major national study of more than 160,000 employers found that widespread racial discrimination continues to affect blacks, Latinos and Asian Americans. The study compared employers in particular industries and communities to determine whether there was widespread disparity between the rates at which some of those firms employed persons of color, when compared to others. If an employer was found to significantly underutilize non-whites in their workforce, relative to the population of qualified persons of color in the community *and* relative to the degree that other firms in the same industry and locale managed to employ them, the study concluded that discrimination was likely the reason. After all, if one is able to find and employ persons of color, there is little reason for one's competitors not to be able to do the same. Even using this ultimately conservative methodology for ferreting out bias,[112] the study found that at least 75,000 establishments nationwide discriminate intentionally against 1.3 million minorities annually. Although there was some good news in the study too—namely, most employers did not appear to engage in overt racist discrimination—several industries were truly egregious in their patterns of unequal treatment, particularly in the medical, drug and other health-related fields.

What's more, this study (conducted by legal scholars Alfred and Ruth Blumrosen) found that for blacks, Latinos and Asian Americans, there was more than a one in three chance that in any given job search they would face discrimination. Nearly 600,000 blacks, more than 275,000 Latinos and roughly 150,000 Asian Americans each year are subjected to job discrimination according to the study, and for about 90 percent of these, the evidence of discrimination is so blatant—in other words, their utilization by certain companies in certain locales is so substantially below the local and industry norm—that the odds of these outcomes being the result of any factor other than racial bias are only about 1 percent.[113]

Other studies have found similar evidence of blatant racial discrimination. And so, according to one now-famous study from economists at MIT and the University of Chicago in 2004, job applicants with "white-sounding names" are about 50 percent more likely to be called back for a job interview than applicants with "black-sounding" names, even when their qualifications are indistinguishable.[114] In this study, the researchers discovered that the value of merely having a white-sounding name was equivalent to being black and having *eight more years of experience* than a white job applicant.

Other research, spearheaded by Princeton sociologist Devah Pager, has found that when equally qualified and matched black, white and Latino male testers are sent to apply for entry-level jobs—and even when these testers have been carefully trained and evince similar communication styles, physical characteristics and demeanor—whites are far more likely to get a callback than applicants of color. Indeed, Pager has found that even white men who claim to have a felony record are slightly more likely to receive a callback than black applicants without such a record.[115] It should be noted that in Pager's studies, three-fourths of the racial disparities that were seen, emerged in the callback phase of the study. This is instructive, since it is precisely this phase where the least personalizing information is available for the applicants, and it is the point at which the ability of applicants to have already made a substantial personal impression is limited. In other words, for disparities to emerge at this stage in the process strongly suggested that employers were making group-based assumptions about applicants, leading them to screen out blacks and screen in whites.[116]

Recent investigations into particular industries have uncovered substantial evidence of ongoing discriminatory barriers for persons of color. For instance, a 2008 study of the advertising industry discovered that racial discrimination is nearly 40 percent more severe in advertising than in the overall U.S. labor market, and that things have actually gotten worse in that industry, relative to the rest of the economy, over the past three decades. According to the study, black college graduates working in the ad industry with the same qualifications as whites earn 20 percent less than their white counterparts. Furthermore, even when they have equal qualifications, blacks are still only about half as likely as whites to serve as advertising managers and professionals. Large ad firms are 60 percent more likely than firms in the overall labor market to employ *no* African Americans at all, and even when blacks are present in such companies, they are more than a third less likely than whites to serve in the more powerful, lucrative and creative positions of such firms.[117]

Another recent study in New York explored racial discrimination in the city's upscale restaurant industry. According to the researchers, when testers were sent out to apply for jobs with equal qualifications, education, language skills, appearance and demeanor, applicants of color were half as likely as whites to get a job offer, and discrimination occurred in roughly a third of all restaurants tested. Employers were far more likely to enthusiastically describe the available jobs to whites, far more often challenged the résumés of applicants of color, offered better shifts and work schedules to whites and offered whites longer and more detailed interviews.[118] Although employers often blamed applicants' accents as the reason they wouldn't hire certain persons of color for jobs as waiters, those same employers showed a persistent preference for white waiters with European accents, suggesting it was less the issue of communication and more the preference for whites in the "front of the house" that dictated their decisions.[119]

Other research has suggested that discrimination is especially persistent in service industry occupations, such as retail establishments. Although some have chalked up inequity in this sector to a skill deficit on the part of blacks—particularly a deficit in so-called "soft skills" concerning communication style—even when researchers have sent out *more* qualified black testers to apply for such jobs, whites were still more likely to be granted an interview than their black counterparts. In situations where only one member of a black-white testing pair received an interview, whites were on the winning end of the equation almost twice as often as blacks despite being less qualified than the persons of color against whom they were competing.[120] This discrimination seems to be especially pernicious in suburbs, where blacks are hired at only half the rate at which they are represented in the applicant pool, and whites are hired at a rate 22 percent greater than their share of suburban job applicants.[121]

Significantly, this last statistic drives a stake through the heart of much of William Julius Wilson's "spatial mismatch" theory. Recall that Wilson's position, articulated consistently for roughly thirty years—and central to the post-racial view of white/black job and income inequality—holds that blacks face worse job and earnings prospects than whites because jobs are mostly in the suburbs, while a disproportionate number of blacks continue to live in urban centers. Thus they are simply unable to access the jobs in the places where the jobs increasingly are emerging. But if blacks *are* attempting to access those jobs and are applying for them with equal qualifications only to be under-hired even relative to their availability, then "spatial mismatch" cannot possibly be the culprit. Either overt employer bias or a kind of indirect bias—for instance, a type that drives employers to attempt to match workers to the racial makeup of their client and customer base—must be considered operative. Indeed, this latter form, whereby business owners prefer whites not because they are more qualified per se, but because they presume (rightly or wrongly) that their customers would prefer to deal with white store clerks, managers, etc. has been observed on several occasions.[122] Discrimination has been found to be substantial in temporary employment agencies as well, in part for the same reason: the perception—often an accurate one—that clients (in this case, employers contracting with the temp service) prefer to hire white workers.[123]

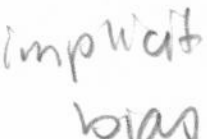

Elsewhere, and even when there is no intent to privilege whites over others, employers may persist in the exclusion of applicants of color by way of hiring networks that are, thanks to past unequal opportunity, disproportionately white. Recent research has found, not surprisingly, that white men receive far better job leads and job-related information from informal networks and word-of-mouth than do either white women or people or color.[124] But while it is well understood that the most lucrative private sector jobs are often filled by way of networking, what is less recognized is how important racially exclusive networking can also be for the landing of blue-collar positions. Research has shown, for instance, that white foremen on construction jobs tend to hire whites they know over blacks they don't, irrespective of actual objective qualifications or experience.[125] Examining white and black men from the same vocational schools, with the same work and educational records, applying for the same jobs, additional research indicates a substantial advantage for whites stemming from greater networking and connections.[126]

In light of the president's economic stimulus plan, which pumped a considerable amount of monies into construction projects from roads and highways to bridge and other infrastructure repair, this tendency for whites to engage in discrimination within the industry should give us pause as to the benefit of colorblind, race-neutral public policy. To lavish funding on these efforts in the name of job creation or retention, as the president did, is to ignore the racially uneven way in which those jobs will likely be filled. To be blind to the way in which the stimulus, in this fashion, may disproportionately benefit whites is to become complicit in the financing of inequality.

Occasionally, even employers who have no intent to discriminate against job applicants of color, may end up treating those applicants unfairly, thanks to the ingrained, if subtle, biases of those charged with evaluating potential employees. Years of research have indicated a tendency for whites to spot merit most quickly in someone who reminds them of themselves, and that members of dominant social groups have a particularly difficult time fairly evaluating the merit of minority group members. Evidence points to a process whereby whites over-remember stereotype-confirming behavior or tendencies in applicants of color, and ignore the same traits in other whites. So, for instance, if a person of color mispronounces a word, ends a sentence with a preposition, or stumbles while speaking during a job interview, it may trigger what psychologists call a mental *schema* (or set of ideas that are linked to one another in memory) regarding stereotypes of inadequate black performance and ability. Yet, if a white job applicant did the very same things, it would not trigger remembrance of a stereotypical and negative schema regarding white people (because there are none when it comes to intelligence), and it would likely be forgotten or never even noticed. Because of this, employers could easily conclude that white applicants were more qualified and better "fits" in a given job complex, even though there is no objective basis for the determination, and even though this conclusion may well have been the result of triggered unconscious biases.[127]

Those who are skeptical of claims of prejudice naturally have a ready set of challenges for those who insist the problem is real. First, they point to immigrant success stories as evidence that the United States is well on the way to becoming a racism-free nation. Yet discrimination against immigrants of color is also widespread.

Indeed, according to research from 2007, when comparing workers of equal productivity, similar occupational status and comparable educational attainment, immigrants with the lightest skin shade earn nearly 20 percent more than immigrants with the darkest skin shades.[128] Second, those who doubt the persistence of racial bias in America often refer to Asian American income data as proof that the United States is an equal opportunity society. But in fact, a closer look at statistics on Asian American income indicates that most are not doing nearly as well as believed. If anything, the data points to continued barriers to equal opportunity for Asian Americans, all claims about their success notwithstanding.

For instance, although median income for Asian Americans is above that of whites, in the aggregate, this is because the Asian American population, on average, has far higher rates of college and post-graduate education than the white population. Because Asian immigration to the United States has been relatively selective, with a disproportionate percentage of Asian immigrants coming with pre-existing educational backgrounds, economic advantages, or the intent to pursue higher education upon arrival, the Asian population as a whole is more highly educated than the white population. As such, they will logically earn more, per capita, than whites with less academic background. But considering how much more education Asian Americans have, on average, relative to their white counterparts, their earnings advantages are much smaller than should be expected.

Whereas fewer than 16 percent of whites had a college degree in 2000, 22.5 percent of Chinese Americans did, as did 31.3 percent of Japanese Americans, 24.4 percent of Korean Americans and Asian Indians, nearly 31 percent of Filipino Americans and

28 percent of Taiwanese Americans. So, although Chinese American income is 17 percent higher than white income, they are 40 percent more likely than whites to have a college degree and 2.3 times more likely to have an advanced degree. Japanese American income is 50 percent higher on average than that for whites; however, Japanese Americans are twice as likely as whites, on average, to have a college degree and 70 percent more likely to have an advanced degree. Asian Indian Americans have 45 percent higher income than whites, on average, but are 60 percent more likely than whites to have a college degree and 3.5 times more likely to have an advanced degree.[129]

In truth, the only statistics that can indicate whether or not Asian Americans truly have equal opportunity are those relating to their earnings, relative to the earnings of whites with the same level of education. And when those comparisons are made, the evidence is clear: Asian Americans earn less than whites with the same educational background in almost every instance. For those without a high school diploma, whites earn 25 percent more than their Asian American counterparts. For those with a diploma but no college degree, whites earn 28 percent more than their Asian American counterparts. For those with a bachelor's degree but no graduate-level degree, whites earn 14 percent more than their Asian American counterparts—about $7,500 more annually. In other words, and despite attempts to use Asian "success" as a way to dismiss the reality of racism and white privilege, the evidence actually makes clear the advantages of being white in the United States and the disadvantages of being Asian American, irrespective of qualifications.[130]

Additionally, the upward skewing of Asian incomes relative

to those of whites is caused by the differential geographic distribution of whites and Asians throughout the United States. Asian Americans are concentrated heavily in the West, which is a higher-income region than other parts of the country. Half of all Asian Americans and Pacific Islanders live in the West (disproportionately in California and Hawaii) compared to less than one-fifth of American whites who do. Conversely, a third of whites live in the lowest-income region, the South, while only 19 percent of Asian Americans do.[131] If one group lives disproportionately in a higher-wage region and another is spread out across the country, naturally the first of these will have higher per capita incomes. But once incomes are examined solely for those whites and Asian Americans living in California, for example, the numbers reverse: Whites earn more than their Asian American counterparts and have much lower poverty rates.[132] When we look only at the poverty rates in those places where Asians are clustered—rather than comparing them with whites spread far and wide in lower-wage regions—we discover that in places like Los Angeles, San Francisco, and even an East Coast metropolis like New York City, Asian American poverty rates are *double* the rates for whites in the same cities.[133]

Sadly, the advocates of post-racial liberalism ignore the copious volumes of research demonstrating ongoing job discrimination against people of color. For instance, Richard Thompson Ford has been dismissive of the previously mentioned study on the way black-named job applicants are treated compared to white-named applicants. Yet his critique of the study suggests that he either failed to understand the research or deliberately deceives about its findings, so as to maintain confidence in his post-racial narrative. First, Ford claims that employers who respond negatively to black-sounding names may simply assume they are less capable or qualified. But the study in question involved equally qualified black-named applicants, whose résumés were every bit as impressive as those of their white-named counterparts. If employers overlook this salient fact all because of a name, then they are making a racially biased assumption, in disregard of the actual evidence before them—evidence they apparently refuse to consider. This is about as close to a textbook definition of racism as one can get.

But Ford goes even further in his cavalier dismissal of this groundbreaking research. Because black comedian Bill Cosby has blasted poor African Americans for giving their children names that are identifiably black, the fact that white employers discriminate against such persons can't be evidence of racism. As Ford explains it: "When Cliff Huxtable can be called a racist, it's probably time to rethink our terms."[134] So if a black person of some notoriety agrees with a racist assumption made regularly by white people, those white people can no longer be thought of as engaging in racism. Which means, by definition, that if even one prominent black person could be found who would defend segregation or enslavement—and of course, such persons existed—neither of those amounted to racism either: a position so intellectually putrid as to merit no further comment.

Racism, Discrimination and Housing

Beyond the realm of employment, there is much evidence to indicate ongoing racial discrimination in housing and mortgage markets. Just as past housing discrimination hampered the ability of black and brown families in mid-century to accumulate assets and wealth, so too, present-day discrimination in housing restricts the ability of younger generations of persons of color to do so. It was 2006, after all, in which the largest number of housing discrimination complaints ever (including race-based complaints) were filed.[135] Studies have estimated that at least 2 million and perhaps as many as 3.7 million instances of race-based housing discrimination against persons of color take place each year.[136] Although sometimes this discrimination manifests as outright denial of rental property or denial of mortgage loans to people of color, far more often it takes the shape of racial "steering" (whereby people are relegated to same-race neighborhoods, no matter their own desires for more integrated spaces), or the offering of housing to people of color on terms far less desirable than the terms offered to whites.

Regarding the current housing meltdown and the ongoing subprime mortgage mess, it was people of color who were disproportionately roped into high-cost loans, made to pay more for properties than they would have been had they been white. By 2006, mortgages sold to Latinos and blacks were 2.5 to 3 times more likely to be subprime than mortgages sold to whites. While these disparities sometimes reflect factors of creditworthiness and collateral, research indicates that persons of color—black, Latino, indigenous and occasionally Asian—are more likely to be steered to a subprime loan at higher cost than are whites with the same income and credit scores. One study in 2006 found that even high-income black and Latino borrowers were more likely than low-income whites to wind up with a high-cost loan,[137] and up to half of the subprime loans given out over the past several years went to persons who could have (and should have) qualified for lower rates.[138] In New York City, as just one example, black households with annual incomes of $68,000 or more are five times more likely to have a subprime mortgage than white households with similar or even less income. On a mid-range loan of $350,000, this means that black borrowers will end up paying, on average, over $250,000 more in interest over the life of the loan than their white counterparts.[139]

Warnings about subprime lending and its consequences for people of color have been sounded for years, with little attention paid until the impacts began to affect the overall economy. It was in the early 2000s, for instance, that the North Carolina–based Community Reinvestment Coalition exposed Citigroup's subprime lender, Citi, for making excess profits on the backs of poor, mostly African American families, ultimately roping into high-cost loans 90,000 borrowers who could have qualified for regular mortgages. These borrowers were then charged so much excess interest that, on average, families would have had to pay more than $100,000 in additional cost over the life of their mortgages. This predatory gouging amounted to over $5.7 billion in excess charges, for the benefit of Citi and to the detriment of the borrowers.[140]

Earlier this year, when the Baltimore NAACP sued Wells Fargo for targeting black communities with subprime loans, former bank employees admitted in court affidavits that loan officers regularly referred to black customers as "mud people," called the loans sold to them "ghetto loans," and offered financial bonuses to loan officers who successfully pushed subprime loans in minority neighborhoods. According to one former employee who had once been Wells Fargo's top-producing subprime loan officer, the bank specifically steered blacks who could have qualified for lower-rate loans into the high-cost instruments. According to the affidavits, loan officers would alter the credit information of black borrowers on their applications and even cut-and-paste bad credit information from one borrower onto the applications of black borrowers with good credit, in order to flip the loan from the prime to the subprime category.[141]

The black and brown face of the subprime lending debacle is not the result of people of color desiring such instruments, nor because laws required the giving of loans to low-income people of color. This latter argument, made often by conservatives, is entirely without merit. Lenders that aren't even covered by fair-lending laws gave out most of the high-cost, risky loans. And loans given out under fair-lending laws like the Community Reinvestment Act actually tend to perform better, and have far lower foreclosure rates than loans written by the largely unregulated mortgage brokers who engaged in predatory lending with abandon.[142] If anything, imposing *more* fair-lending regulations and extending those regulations to all lending institutions (which, by definition would have required a rejection of post-racial rhetoric and race-blind/racism-blind policy making) could have helped prevent at least some of the current housing crisis.

Additionally, the colorblind approach to dealing with racial disparities in housing—which seeks to treat the matter as one of class inequity alone, in which "concentrated poverty" is viewed as a separate phenomenon, apart from racism—is inadequate, given the ongoing barriers to housing access faced by even those persons of color who are not poor. So, for instance, affluent black households are every bit as racially isolated (in black and heavily poor areas) as poor blacks are.[143] And whereas having greater levels of education and higher incomes tends to correlate with living in neighborhoods with lower crime rates and higher property values when one is white, this correlation disappears for blacks.[144] Even with greater economic and educational success, ongoing housing discrimination blocks blacks from the housing they might well procure were they simply white.

The most recent study (as of this writing), conducted in Pittsburgh, found that even when black families have better credit, higher incomes, more savings and less debt than white families applying for loans, they are likely to be discriminated against. In the study in question, black applicants were treated worse than their white counterparts nearly 60 percent of the time. They were more likely to be actively discouraged by the lender and told they would not be able to afford a home, and were given less information about loans or home availability. In addition, black testers were quoted an interest rate a full quarter-point higher than their *less*-qualified white counterparts, on average.[145]

Racism, Discrimination and Education

Closely related to the matter of housing inequity, educational inequity continues to plague the lives of millions of students of color. Though working-class and low-income students of all colors face inadequate educational resources due to economic status alone, explicitly racial forms of marginalization are very much in play for non-whites, above and beyond class standing. To the extent children of color and their families too often live in residentially isolated communities where rates of poverty are higher—and this because of race-based discrimination in housing over many generations—black and Latino kids face the double-whammy of economic and racial marginalization in schools located in those communities.

Young people face intense racial and economic segregation in America today. About 70 percent of students of color attend majority-minority schools, half of all black students are in schools that are at least three-fourths people of color, and a third of both blacks and Latinos attend schools where the student bodies are virtually all black and brown.[146] In large urban areas, these data are even more extreme. So, for instance, in Chicago, the average black student attends an 86 percent black school, while in New York City, six in ten black students attend a school where 90 percent or more of all students are black.[147] In large urban areas generally, two-thirds of black and Latino students attend schools where enrollment is at least 90 percent black and brown.[148] These majority–people of color schools are anywhere from eleven to thirteen times more likely than mostly white schools to be places with high levels of concentrated poverty among their students.[149] Concentrated poverty then complicates the task of delivering a high-quality education to students, as their families will face disproportionate rates of unemployment, inadequate nutrition and growing up in isolated, crowded spaces, largely cut off from the larger social opportunity structure.

The effects of being concentrated in such schools cannot be overstated. First, it is often lower-income schools of color in which the least experienced teachers are placed, as those with more experience seek out teaching assignments in wealthier and whiter communities. In fact, recent research has found that independent of neighborhood factors and quality, teachers with the most experience, highest levels of certification and best track records in terms of boosting the achievement of their students, choose to leave schools when the numbers of black students enrolled begin to increase.[150] In California, schools where more than half the teachers lack credentials in the fields they teach have, on average, 98 percent students of color.[151] Because the most experienced teachers often have tenure and power within the teachers' unions, they are able to get placement in other communities, in whiter schools, while less experienced and younger teachers get placed in the schools with the greatest challenges. So nationally, in schools serving mostly people of color, students have less than a fifty-fifty chance of ending up with a math or science teacher with a degree in the field, or who is licensed to teach those subjects specifically. And new teachers at mostly black and brown schools are five times more likely to be unlicensed in the field they teach than are newly hired teachers in mostly white schools. Overall, students of color are half as likely as white students to be taught by the most experienced and qualified teachers, and twice as likely to be taught by the least experienced and least qualified teachers.[152]

Exposure to low-quality educational resources, as so often occurs in hyper-segregated schools, can then have a profound effect on cognitive development. Indeed, children can lose several points on a standard IQ test for every year they are subjected to substandard resources, instruction and facilities.[153] As for exposure to less-qualified teachers, this too has a specific and deleterious impact on students of color. Research from Texas shows that students who start out ahead academically but are then exposed to less-qualified teachers experience a rapid drop in performance, while those who start out behind but have highly qualified instruction can catch up with those who started ahead, and even surpass them.[154]

It should be noted that the concentration of students of color in high-density, majority-minority and low-income schools is not only an issue for poor and working-class students and families of

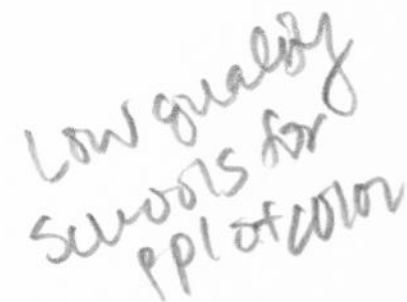

color, however. Indeed, even blacks with incomes higher than those of whites are less likely to attend high-quality schools and more likely to live in low-income neighborhoods than whites are.[155] According to one study in Philadelphia, African American children from affluent families typically attend schools with three times as many low-achieving poor students as affluent white children do.[156] To the extent the concentration of poverty has tended to have a racialized face—specifically a black and brown one—it seems unlikely that mere universal programs of educational uplift could address the persistent inequities that result. Even if educational policy were reformed overnight, such that additional monies were pumped into all schools that were struggling, the racial gaps created by residential segregation and selective teacher assignments would likely persist.

In keeping with the notion that race-specific injury confounds the ability of colorblind universalism to rectify persistent racial inequities in the realm of education, consider the evidence of discriminatory treatment in schools themselves. Research has found that students of color, especially African Americans, are disproportionately likely to be classified and labeled as learning disabled and placed in special education programs. This is especially the case for more subjective categories of disorder and disability, like emotional disturbance, rather than for medically diagnosable disabilities. The tendency to categorize students of color in this way owes less to genuinely greater levels of disorder in such students than to the racial dynamics of the schools they attend. For instance, in Arizona public schools, males of color at mostly white schools are two-thirds more likely to be labeled as emotionally disturbed or learning disabled than minority males at mostly minority schools, even though the latter are far more likely to have grown up in poverty, and thus could be expected to occasionally demonstrate emotional or cognitive impairment. This suggests that at whiter schools, teachers are more apt to see dysfunction in black and brown students, not because they necessarily demonstrate more of it, but because of the teachers' own inabilities to relate to the students of color, or because of various subconscious biases.[157]

Nationally, black students are anywhere from 1.5 times to four times more likely than whites to be classified as mentally handicapped or emotionally disturbed: a range so broad as to suggest significant imprecision, subjectivity and likely bias in the evaluation process.[158] After all, why would one state have a ratio of impaired black students that was four times the rate for whites, while another state, possibly next door, would only have a ratio of 1.5 to one?

This labeling of students has a profound effect on their future educational attainment. Indeed, students labeled as learning disabled are 20 percent more likely to drop out than students not labeled in this way, and those labeled emotionally disturbed are three times more likely to quit school than students with physical disabilities.[159] Although the labeling itself is not the cause of the students' failure to complete their schooling, it creates a set of expectations and stigmas for those so labeled that can suppress the drive to achieve academically. Nationally, for instance, research has found that students labeled as mentally handicapped or emotionally disturbed are likely to be placed in restricted learning environments, despite evidence indicating that such students need exactly the opposite in order to thrive. And once labeled and removed from normal classroom environments, students of color receive less intensive services and support than whites who have been similarly labeled.[160]

Although it might be easy to attribute the mistreatment in these cases to class factors, rather than race—and thus to assume that colorblind universalism might be sufficient for addressing the issue—the research has found that students of color who are not poor and live in affluent districts are far more likely to be labeled mentally handicapped or emotionally disturbed than their white classmates. Furthermore, the over-diagnosis appears only in the entirely subjective arenas of intellectual capacity and emotional disturbance, rather than in the areas of specific learning disabilities or medically supportable diagnoses, suggesting that much of the classification process is imprecise and given to tacit if not explicit racial bias.

Likewise, and in keeping with this notion that disability labeling can become a self-fulfilling prophecy, consider the practice and impact of so-called academic "ability tracking." On the one hand, studies have long found that blacks and Latinos are far more likely than white students to be placed in lower-track remedial-level classes and far less likely to be placed in honors courses than whites, even when their prior academic performance would justify different placement.[161] Oftentimes, this placement is due to structural inequities such as the fact that schools attended mostly by students of color are much less likely to have advanced placement (AP) or honors courses offered. Nationally, schools disproportionately serving students of color have about one-third as many advanced courses offered, per capita, as schools serving mostly whites.[162] In California, for instance, there are more than 125 high schools without a single AP class. Overwhelmingly, these schools serve student bodies that are mostly black and brown.[163] This disparity in secondary schools further promotes racial inequity in higher education as well. So, for instance, as of the late 1990s the median grade-point average of entering first-year students at UCLA was 4.15 on a standard 4-point scale. Of course, the only way to receive a GPA of more than 4.0 is to earn a bonus by taking AP classes. Which means that there are thousands of black and Latino kids in California who have no chance to earn the kind of GPA received by the typical white student at UCLA, no matter how hard they work, simply because of the unavailability of such classes in their schools.[164]

Significantly, evidence suggests that ability tracking actually hampers the literacy and academic accomplishments of students of color at lower levels of prior ability, while failing to boost the performance of more advanced students. In other words, tracking fails to deliver the benefits it promises, either for those at the bottom or those at the top of the academic spectrum.[165] Indeed, those labeled as slower learners often suffer from reduced self-esteem and a lowered sense of their own efficacy, which compromises their academic success and creates a self-fulfilling prophecy of sorts, whereby their track becomes their destiny in school.[166]

Those assigned to teach lower-track students actually admit their own low expectations for the children in their academic care. As Jeannie Oakes noted in her classic text on the subject, low-track teachers typically eschew a focus on academic advancement or mastery of material for their students, focusing instead on maintaining discipline, respect for authority, punctuality and simple task completion. Furthermore, they emphasize how to be less outspoken and more compliant with rules and regulations as set by authority figures (be they teachers or future bosses). There is very little room within remedial-track classes for development of critical thinking skills or for moving up the school ladder.[167]

Students tracked lower also receive less direct instruction than their higher-tracked counterparts. Higher-tracked English students spend about 15 percent more time receiving direct instruction than students in lower tracks, while higher-tracked math students spend about 22 percent more time receiving instruction than those in lower-tracked math classes. In all, the instructional differences amount to nearly forty hours less actual instruction for those in lower-tracked classes each year.[168] Students of color, who are being shunted into these remedial-level classes most often, are thus being deprived of the ability to learn, and the gap between them and their whiter counterparts in advanced classes continues to grow.

Although the premise of "No Child Left Behind" (the Bush administration's signature education bill) is that racial achievement gaps should be closed completely within ten years, the legislation never came with the kind of resource supports needed to make that goal achievable. Although No Child Left Behind requires certain outcomes, it does not mandate that schools must equalize the resources available to all students in order to make those more equitable outcomes likely. Nor did the law—which has so far been continued under the Obama administration, with very little functional change in its specific policy formulations—seek to put an end to the pernicious tracking practices in our schools that all but *guarantee* the leaving behind of children. In fact, many states have adopted norm-referenced tests as determinants of their "annual yearly progress" (mandated by the law), failing to appreciate that

norm-referenced tests *by definition* produce a distribution where half of all test-takers will fall below the 50-percentile mark and thus be considered below average.[169] In other words, tests that mandate failure and inequity in achievement are being used under a law intended to promote success and reduce inequity! To advocate equity but maintain structures that, by definition, create inequity is the ultimate contradiction.

As a result of No Child Left Behind, schools have been under intense pressure to meet federal guidelines for test scores, so as not to be sanctioned by the Department of Education. This pressure has been especially intense for schools serving mostly students of color, causing many such schools to emphasize teaching to the test, simply to meet federal and even state standards, rather than teaching the kinds of high-level materials given to students in suburbs and private schools.[170] High-stakes testing has also created incentives for schools to push lower-achieving students out, rather than keep them in the schools, attempt to educate them and suffer the possible penalty if they fail, in terms of meeting testing requirements.[171] In Chicago, for instance, schools have been expelling low-achieving students even by the age of 16, under the pretense that their academic achievement or attendance records make it unlikely that they would graduate by the age of 21. Rather than resolve to educate such students—almost all of whom are students of color—the schools give up, remove the students and thus boost their test-score profile as a result, with blacks banished from the schools at three times the rate of whites or Latinos.[172]

In post-Katrina New Orleans, supposedly "open enrollment" charter schools—intended to inject competition into the city's previously failing school system and lauded as having done so—have been pre-screening students to determine which of them are unlikely to pass a state required test the following year. Then the students who fail in the pre-test are pushed out, so as to protect the school's test scores in line with state and federal mandates. Others have counseled parents of lower-achieving students, or those with inconsistent attendance, to voluntarily withdraw from charter schools or face expulsion. Once these students are removed, the charters are left with the supposedly "better" students, which allows them to meet federal and state standards by selecting their student bodies. Needless to say, virtually all students being pushed out are black.[173]

Also under No Child Left Behind, schools must demonstrate the elimination of performance gaps between those who have limited English proficiency (LEP) and those for whom English is their native language. Although this is an admirable goal, it cannot be met in most cases for one simple reason: namely, in most districts, once students demonstrate English proficiency, they are removed from the LEP group and their scores are no longer considered part of the LEP group averages. Thus, by definition, the only persons remaining in the LEP group will be those who are *not* proficient in the language of the test, and who therefore will not likely perform well on it.[174]

In addition to unequal instruction and regulations under No Child Left Behind that all but ensure disparate racial outcomes in schooling, there is also a substantial amount of evidence demonstrating profoundly unequal discipline meted out to students of color as compared to whites. Nationally, fourteen separate studies have found clear racial disparities in rates of suspension and expulsion from school. Black students are two to three times more likely to be suspended or expelled than whites, even though they do not, contrary to popular belief, violate school rules disproportionately, relative to white students.[175] Indeed, when it comes to some of the most serious school rule infractions, whites often lead the pack, and they certainly violate those rules at least as often as black and brown students do, from possession of drugs to drinking and smoking.[176] Most of the infractions for which students of color are punished are vague, highly subjective offenses—far more given to interpretation and thus implicit bias on the part of teachers—such as "disrespect for authority," "making excessive noise" or loitering.[177]

Significantly, the research suggests that unequal discipline is not due to mere class bias against lower-income students. In fact, even when comparing only blacks and whites of the same economic status, black students face disproportionate suspensions and expulsions relative to rates of misbehavior. As Russell Skiba, a professor at Indiana University, notes:

> Contrary to the socioeconomic hypothesis, the current investigation demonstrates that significant racial disparities in school discipline remain even after controlling for socioeconomic status. In this sample, an index of socioeconomic status had virtually no effect when used as a covariate in a test of racial differences in office referrals and suspensions. Indeed, disciplinary disproportionality by socioeconomic status appears to be a somewhat *less* robust finding than gender or racial disparity.[178]

As with so much of the evidence regarding racial inequity in the educational system, this suggests that colorblind universalism as a way to reduce racial disparities will prove inadequate. There is simply too much race-specific injury occurring to allow for post-racialism (at the level of ideology or policy) to suffice. Unfortunately, teachers often go out of their way to be colorblind—or what educational theorist Mica Pollock calls "colormute"—by failing to discuss race, or even to use basic and benign racial descriptors to describe their students. As a result, educators replicate inequities by failing to get to the bottom of their own biases or the structural impediments to equal opportunity within their schools.[179]

Racism, Discrimination and Health Care

Just as racial disparity exists in income, wealth and educational attainment, so too in terms of basic health there are large and seemingly intractable gaps between whites and people of color. Whether regarding life expectancy, infant mortality rates, rates of low birth weight for newborns or the rates at which adults die from largely preventable diseases, whites are in far better shape than those who are black or brown. Indeed, it is estimated that nearly 100,000 blacks die each year who wouldn't, if black mortality rates were equal to those of whites.[180]

In addressing these racial disparities, there are largely three schools of thought as to both the diagnosis of the problem, and the recommendations put forward for solving it. The first argues that racial health gaps are largely the result of economic inequity. According to this line of reasoning, people of color, especially African Americans, disproportionately populate the bottom of the class structure; thus, since poorer people typically have worse health than the more affluent, black/white differences in health outcomes will manifest. The second school of thought argues that differential health outcomes reflect different lifestyles and choices made by whites as opposed to people of color: If blacks engage in less healthy lifestyles (worse diets, less exercise, etc.), they will naturally have worse health outcomes. And finally, some argue that racial disparities in health reflect a bit of economic and behavioral factors, but also racism itself: first, the health effects of society-wide racism and discrimination, which accumulate over time, and second, racially disparate treatment by physicians themselves, even those with no intent to injure people of color but who are influenced, like everyone else, by implicit biases.

Post-racial liberalism typically embraces one of the first two explanations, and occasionally a combination of those two. Its proponents argue that blacks and other people of color are victims of bad economic status and are less likely to have health insurance coverage (especially high-quality preventive care through an employer, for instance), and so this can explain much of the racial health gap. They further suggest that lifestyle choices regarding food and exercise play a role in worse health outcomes for people of color. As candidate Obama himself said on the campaign trail, black folks need more exercise and access to fresh food in their neighborhoods. By and large the president has eschewed any direct discussion of racial gaps and strategies for closing them, however. When asked the question directly, as he was in the summer of 2008 while still campaigning, he deftly pivoted back to the need for universal coverage. And in his book *The Audacity of Hope* he insisted that universal coverage would do more to reduce racial disparities in health than any race-targeted effort ever could.

But despite his insistence and optimism about the efficacy of universal and colorblind public policy to solve race-specific injury, there is reason to believe that such an approach will fall well short of its proclaimed benefits (and this, assuming universal coverage will even be implemented, which at the time of this writing seems a remote possibility at best).

Contrary to popular belief, racial disparities in health outcomes are not merely, or even mostly, about disparities in income or health care coverage. Indeed, some of the largest racial gaps—especially, for instance, for hypertension—manifest at the upper end of the income spectrum, between whites and blacks that have high incomes and occupational status, college degrees and good health insurance.[181] Among the indicators that racial health gaps are about more than mere economics and health care affordability—and thus that universal coverage is inadequate to the task of remedying them—consider:

- Black women with a bachelor's or higher-level degree have a higher rate of infant mortality for their newborns and infants than white women who dropped out before entering high school.[182] When comparing black and white women with college degrees, the infant mortality rate for children born to black women is nearly *three times* higher than the rate for children born to similar white women.[183]

- Black households with annual incomes of $35,000 or more have higher rates of infant mortality than white households with annual incomes of less than $10,000.[184]

- Black women who received early prenatal care have infant mortality rates that are nearly double the rate for white women who received late *or no* prenatal care at all.[185]

- White women who start out in life poor but move up the ladder show improved birth outcomes for their children, while black mothers largely see no improvement in outcome, even if they are upwardly mobile. Likewise, as Latina immigrant moms remain in the United States and improve their economic condition, their health declines; and South Asian Indian women with economic profiles similar to white women nonetheless have birth outcomes for their kids (low birth weight and infant mortality) comparable to those of poor black women.[186]

Significantly, these racial gaps are not due to behavioral or lifestyle differences or genetic factors specific to black women and their children. Even black women who don't smoke, for instance, have higher rates of infant mortality for their children than white women who *do* smoke, and foreign-born blacks (including continental Africans) have infant mortality rates and rates of low–birth weight babies that are far lower than their African American counterparts, and in line with white averages.[187] But once African women immigrate to the United States, within one generation, their daughters have a much higher risk of pre-term and/or low–birth weight babies, approaching the elevated levels for other African American women.[188] Likewise, although black immigrants from majority-black nations and regions of the world come to the United States on balance healthier than blacks from mostly white areas (or the United States itself), after a short time in America, their health status erodes and drops to match that of less healthy blacks.[189] This too suggests that there is something about being black in the United States, and not something about blackness biologically, that explains disparate health outcomes.

So what is it about the experience of being black in the United States that seems to make such a difference in the health outcomes experienced by African Americans as opposed to whites? Typically there are two explanations: the effects of discrimination on black health over time, in a variety of settings; and differential treatment at the hands of physicians.

In the past several years, more than a hundred studies have found a relationship between racial discrimination and negative physical health outcomes for people of color. Research has found that experiences with racial discrimination increase stress levels among persons of color, thereby elevating blood pressure and correlating directly with worse health.[190] Being the target of racial bigotry causes the brain's hypothalamus to send an alert to the adrenal glands, resulting in a release of adrenaline along with the release of endorphins in the brain and cortisol (a stress-related hormone) throughout the body. Over time, these experiences can damage the hypothalamic-pituitary-adrenal (HPA) axis.[191] As the research explains:

> A normally functioning HPA systematically releases appropriate amounts of adrenaline and cortisol to address the threat of stress. In contrast, when the HPA has been overloaded by ongoing, durable experiences of racial discrimination, the intermittent release of adrenaline and cortisol can cause harm. An excess of adrenaline may cause surges

> in blood pressure that, in turn, cause scars in arteries where plaque can build and hamper the flow of blood throughout the body, thus increasing the risk of heart attack, stroke, and/or heart disease. In short, chronic exposure to racial discrimination may damage the HPA axis so severely that the secretion of cortisol and adrenaline are never again normal.[192]

Researchers have developed a theory to explain the unique effects of race-related stress on women of color and the association between that stress and pre-term birth and low birth weight. To wit, the concept of the *allostatic load*, which refers to the cumulative physiological burden imposed by excess stress:

> It may be that the standard set of socioeconomic factors fails to explain the full meaning of being African-American. . . . Experiences of being discriminated against as a person of color are everyday occurrences at once painful and threatening. This chronic strain may have an effect more insidious and powerful than is captured by our customary models. . . . The hypothesis that a woman's experience of chronic threat before pregnancy affects pregnancy outcome rests on the concept of allostatic load. . . . [Allostasis] refers to the ability of the body to achieve stability through change, such that the autonomic nervous system, the hypothalamic-pituitary-adrenal (HPA) axis, and cardiovascular, metabolic, and immune systems protect the body by responding to internal and external stress. The price of this accommodation to stress can be allostatic load, which is the wear-and-tear from chronic overactivity or underactivity of the allostatic system.

> We theorize that frequent stress whether concurrent, feared, or remembered, increases allostatic load. Thus, we propose that a woman's chronic exposure to racism or violence creates an allostatic load that imprints itself upon her HPA axis prior to conception, altering the endocrine milieu in which the placenta is established, and potentially changing the hormonal interaction between fetus, placenta and mother.[193]

Studies of allostatic load markers (including levels of epinephrine and cortisol, which are released in response to stress, as well as blood pressure levels and levels of glycated hemoglobin), have found that blacks in all age groups have evidence of elevated allostatic loading, with young black adults nearly 1.5 times more likely to demonstrate a high score on measures of allostatic load, and blacks 55 to 64 about 2.3 times more likely than their white counterparts to demonstrate this level of stress loading. Interestingly, poor whites display lower scores on measures of allostatic load than non-poor blacks, suggesting that the racial differences in high stress effects are not the result of economic disparity but rather are related to race-specific stresses experienced by people of color, irrespective of class status.[194]

There is an increasing body of medical literature to suggest that this "weathering" effect, which comes from steady and repeated exposure to racial mistreatment, begins to affect people of color at very young ages, first as they learn of the attitudes that are commonly held about their group by members of the dominant society, then as they become exposed to acts of discrimination. In children, this stress can decrease self-esteem and foster anger, depression and even violent acting out. When these stresses accumulate over time, the impact on the physical, mental and emotional health of those experiencing the stress can be dramatic, and can prime the body for all kinds of debilitating conditions later in life.[195] Indeed, the cumulative effect helps explain why racial differences in hypertension begin to dramatically emerge after the age of 30.[196]

Camara P. Jones, MD, a director of research at the Centers for Disease Control, explains:

> By the time you get into the 25–44-year-old group you start to see changes. We have evidence that in white folks, blood pressure is dropping at night, but not in black people. . . . There's a kind of stress, like you're gunning your cardiovascular engine constantly if you're black, that results from dealing with people who are underestimating you, limiting your options. . . . It results from little things like going to a store and if there are two people at the counter—one black and one white—the white person will be first approached. If you have stress from other sources, like a bad marriage, it's not something you think about constantly. But the stresses associated with racism are chronic and unrelenting.

The kind of daily indignities to which people of color are exposed were discussed by black women in a focus group filmed as part of the California Newsreel documentary *Unnatural Causes*.[197] The women, brought together by researchers at Emory University, explained:

> I think constantly, having to internalize the racism that we experience every day. It's like, to me, where do you escape to?

> My daughter, she's real open and friendly, and so, you know, she'll run up to the white children and say, "Can I play with you?" And then they don't even answer; they just look at her and run away. It's heartbreaking for me to see that.

> You have a doctor that comes in that doesn't really pay attention to what it is you're saying, that invalidates what it is you're saying.

> No matter how many times I made it to the final interview, or how many programs come out of my research, it's just not enough. And I think it's unfortunate, but it does something to me internally. I've taken jobs, I mean, getting paid way less than the people that I know don't have as much education. I don't know what kind of résumé to write at this point. So, you know, I'm scared to give people a résumé.

Likewise, a recent report on black male college graduates, who are experiencing elevated levels of unemployment well above those of their white counterparts, noted how many such men are changing their names to sound less identifiably black, or altering their résumés to remove any references that might tip off potential employers to their race. They recount experiences of obtaining interviews from enthusiastic firms, only to watch their chances evaporate as soon as they walk in the room and the prospective employers see the color of their skin.[198] This kind of racial incident, subtle though it may be—and none of the men claim to have been the targets of overt or hostile racism in these cases—can have a terrible impact. In fact, studies have found that overt racism is actually

less distressing, mentally, than more subtle forms of bias. When the brain has to expend valuable cognitive resources merely determining whether or not a racially discriminatory act has occurred, there is more stress associated with the process than in those cases where the cognitive analysis of a situation is far easier.[199]

Although there are certainly class-related forces that add to stress levels and the allostatic load of marginalized persons, the special marginalization experienced by persons of color exacts a unique toll as well. Indeed, the impact of racial discrimination, independent of these other factors like economic or lifestyle variables, has as much, if not more impact on blood pressure than smoking, lack of exercise and a high-fat, high-sodium diet.[200] Additionally, research by Sherman James of Duke University indicates a tendency for persons exposed to racism to resort to what is known as high-effort coping, meaning exerting additional and special effort to prove one's competence, over and above existing racist stereotypes.[201] Although this kind of response to mistreatment might seem laudable—indeed it conjures long-worn social tropes about hard work and initiative, and refusing to be a victim—it comes with a cost. Having to be "twice as good" to get half as far, even when one manages to pull it off, can easily devolve into a real-life "John Henryism," in which, like the folk legend about the steel-driving man who wanted to prove he could pound rail ties as well as a machine, individuals who fall prey to it prove themselves, only to die early from over-stress. Again, this suggests that colorblind universalism will prove inadequate for eliminating racial health disparities, since such a large portion of that disparity is due to experiences with racism itself.

In addition to the effects of racism on black and brown health generally, there is also a growing body of evidence to suggest that patients of color receive unequal and discriminatory treatment at the hands of physicians, making colorblind universalism even more inadequate for narrowing racial health gaps. For instance, when comparing only Medicare patients of the same age, gender and income, African American women are 25 percent less likely to receive mammography screening, and even when comparing patients of the same age, gender and severity of disease, living in the same geographic location and with the same access to cardiac facilities, blacks are 60 percent less likely to be referred for, and to receive coronary angioplasty or bypass surgery.[202] A 2005 study found that black cardiac patients are less likely than whites to receive particular lifesaving interventions, even when all patients are on Medicare and indistinguishable in other background characteristics. In another study in 2007, researchers at Harvard gave doctors a hypothetical vignette in which a patient with chest pain comes to the hospital and is found to have suffered a heart attack. When the vignette was matched with a picture of a black male patient, the doctors were much less likely to recommend lifesaving drugs than when the picture of the "patient" was white.[203] In a review of studies comparing the quality of cardiac care received by white and black patients, the Kaiser Family Foundation and the American College of Cardiology Foundation found that out of eighty-one such studies, nearly seventy indicated that blacks received inferior treatment.[204] Another study by researchers from the University of Washington looked at patients in 1,500 different physicians' practices and found a significant difference in the way white doctors communicated with patients of color, the kind of treatment they recommended and the degree to which they coordinated care regimens with their patients, especially with Asian Pacific Islanders. These differences persisted even when the patients had the same kind of insurance and other background factors.[205]

Though there is little evidence to suggest a significant degree of overt racial bias on the part of physicians—no more nor less, for example, than in the general population—there is research suggesting a substantial amount of subconscious racial bias in favor of whites and against blacks. For instance, research from Harvard medical school tested physicians for unconscious bias and the extent to which that bias predicted differential treatment of white and black patients. The results were clear: There was a substantial degree of implicit bias among white physicians, and this bias was directly correlated with greater levels of disparate treatment of patients.[206] An additional study presented doctors with videos of actors whom they believed to be real patients. Some of the actor/patients were black and others were white. They presented the same symptoms, had the same background characteristics, and in every way but race were indistinguishable. Yet when asked to reflect on the "patients," the doctors said they perceived those who were black to be less intelligent, less likely to fully participate in treatment and more likely to miss scheduled appointments. They also perceived the black actor/patients as less likely than whites to benefit from various invasive procedures, even though the symptoms for both the black and white actor-patients were identical.[207]

Between 2004 and 2006, tests were administered to more than 2,500 doctors to test for implicit racial bias. The outcome demonstrated that white, Latino and Asian physicians have significant implicit pro-white, anti-black biases, while black physicians present no consistent evidence of racial bias.[208] Importantly, implicit biases were two to three times more prevalent than self-reported and overt biases, suggesting that there is a substantial difference between how people portray themselves (and perhaps think of themselves) and the way their minds actually work when it comes to race.

Obviously, if physicians are dispensing unequal and discriminatory care, especially as the result of implicit and subconscious biases, colorblind universalism cannot possibly remedy the problem. Even if health care access were made more affordable and universal coverage the norm, if patients of color are treated differently, and worse than whites, the cost of the care received won't matter much: Cheaper racist care is still racist care. Likewise, if people of color are being battered by racism in other realms of everyday life, the fact that they will have health care coverage and be able to see a doctor when they need one will hardly change the fact that their health will continue to suffer. They'll have access to physicians, but they'll also need them far more often.

None of this is to say that universal health care coverage is unimportant. Nor is it to suggest that addressing basic economic inequities or even personal unhealthy behaviors is not important. All of these are vital aspects of improving the health of the American people. But unless we also address the specific racial components of ill health, from discriminatory care delivery to the effects of racism in society generally (and the next chapter will discuss some ways to do this), racial disparities will remain intact.

In fact, the issues of racism, economic inequity and personal behaviors are more interrelated than we might at first believe. After all, even when racial health gaps are related to economic disparities between whites and blacks, those disparities often have race-specific roots. So, for instance, residential isolation of African

Americans in highly concentrated, poorer neighborhoods has a direct relationship to inferior health outcomes for blacks, due to the health effects of living in older buildings with bad insulation, poor weatherization, lead paint exposure and exposure to other toxins.[209] But that isolation is the result of race-specific barriers to housing access in whiter, more affluent communities, such as overt discrimination or more subtle steering practices. To solve racial disparities related to geographic concentration of blacks in congested urban spaces, policy makers will have to address the uniquely racial barriers to full and equal housing access. Merely having a job or having health care coverage will not address those kinds of problems. Increasingly, medical experts recognize the importance of looking specifically at the impacts of racism on racial health disparities. As Vickie and Brenda Shavers explain in the *Journal of the National Medical Association*:

> The failure to address differences in the behavior towards and opportunities afforded to racial/ethnic minorities contributes to the inability to eliminate racial/ethnic disparities in health. Too often, programs designed to eliminate disparities focus on educating the community without regard for their environment and other circumstances that restrict their freedom of choice and opportunities. Addressing racism as it relates to racial/ethnic health disparities requires an assessment of its prevalence and an understanding of the specific manner in which it operates, not only in the social environment, but in healthcare delivery systems as well.[210]

Likewise, when health gaps are, in part, due to behavioral

and lifestyle differences, these too may be rooted in experiences with racial discrimination. For instance, multiple studies have found that detrimental and high-risk behaviors such as drug use, cigarette smoking, violence and alcohol consumption are directly correlated with being victimized by racism.[211] So addressing the health consequences of these behaviors and "choices" will require more than just a focus on the behavior itself; it will necessitate an examination of the social determinants of those choices, which is to say, a race-conscious approach.

DISPENSING WITH VICTIM-BLAMING: THE INADEQUACY OF CULTURE-OF-POVERTY THINKING

Unfortunately this last admonition—to examine the social determinants of individual and group behaviors—is something of a rarity in the modern era. Instead, conservatives and far too many "post-racial" liberals (like William Julius Wilson, for instance) are given to criticizing people of color, especially those with low income, for what they perceive to be pathological and deviant cultural norms: from single-parenting, to de-emphasizing the importance of education, to welfare dependency. Because of these behavioral norms, African Americans remain behind white families in terms of well-being, or so the theory goes. More than racism and discrimination, cultural norms within black and brown communities are the cause of ongoing racial disparities, according to this view.

While the liberal version of this argument tends to be more forgiving than the conservative version—it at least recognizes that cultural norms have a material basis and can be directly influenced by access to the opportunity structure, or the lack thereof—both versions largely blame racial inequities on the behavior of those victimized by the racial caste system. However much more ecumenical it may sound when compared to the right-wing version of the same argument, it is still a narrative that blames those on the bottom of the class and caste hierarchy for being there.

And as with the conservative culture-of-poverty analysis, the liberal version is filled with inaccuracies. Whether from Moynihan, Wilson, Ford or Obama—all of whom have articulated one or another aspect of the behavioral narrative as a way to explain racial inequities—the argument essentially boils down to this: Black families, because of a history of racist oppression, have adapted to their conditions in ways that are often dysfunctional. According to this perspective, black families are far too accepting of single parenthood, black children and families place too little emphasis on education, and they are too willing to live on public assistance, as opposed to working for a living. To hear the advocates of this argument tell it, if black behavioral norms were more like those of whites, much of the racial disparity written up to discrimination would vanish.

But in fact, changes in the structure of the black family are not the reason for the rise in racial inequity: Indeed, according to a study in the 1990s by the President's Council of Economic Advisors, even if black family structure had not changed at all since the late 1960s, at least 80 percent of the existing income and poverty-rate differences between whites and blacks would have remained the same.[212] Even when black folks are married, racial gaps in well-being remain significant. According to U.S. Census data, black married couples are nearly twice as likely as their white counterparts to be poor, and Latino married couples are more than *four times* as likely as white married couples to be poor.[213] And black and Latina single mothers are 2.5 times as likely to be poor as white single mothers.[214] Likewise, racial disparities in school achievement remain roughly the same, regardless of single-parent household status, once we compare families of like economic condition.[215] In other words, it is not single-parenthood per se, or a lack of "intact" two-parent homes that explains the relative deprivation experienced by persons of color in the United States.

Although it is true that rates of out-of-wedlock childbirth in the black community have increased dramatically since the 1960s, this fact has nothing to do with a change in the sexual behaviors of black men and women, or a cultural pathology regarding "responsible" and "irresponsible" procreative activity. Indeed, the increase in the rate of out-of-wedlock childbirth is almost entirely the result of one factor: namely, the drop in childbirth rates among married black women.[216] Since married black couples are having far fewer children than in past generations, the *percentage* of births in the black community that will end up being to single moms will go up, even though fertility rates have barely budged, and in some cases have dropped precipitously among African American women. It is not that single black women are having more babies than ever before; it is that married black women are having fewer. Thus, as a percentage of the whole, the share that represents so-called illegitimacy will rise. But this says nothing about cultural pathology; it is a mere statistical artifice. Additionally, part of the apparent increase in out-of-wedlock childbirth among black women is due to a change in the way the Census Bureau does its accounting. Prior to the 1980s, single mothers living in extended family

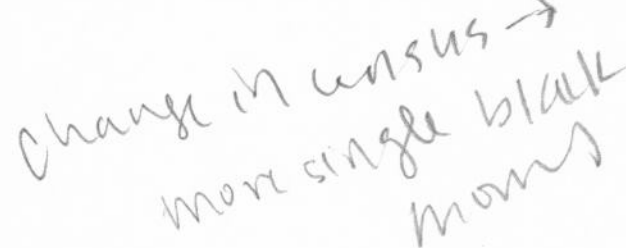

arrangements—for instance, with their own parents or other relatives—were not counted separately by the Census as single mothers with kids. Since that time, however, they have been counted separately, thereby causing the numbers of black single moms to suddenly "explode," even though this increase is due not to actual behavioral changes over time but merely to a bureaucratic alteration in the way the government counts its citizens.[217]

As for the notion that black families and culture place too little emphasis on education—an argument made often to explain higher dropout rates for African Americans, or worse educational performance—this too is an argument rooted more in myth than fact. To begin with, once family economic background is held constant (so that we are only comparing like families, in terms of income and asset status), blacks are actually *more likely* than whites to finish high school and equally likely to finish college—certainly not evidence that blacks as a group place too little emphasis on schooling. In other words, whatever gaps in graduation rates we see are *entirely* the result of economic status factors, not a difference in values vis-à-vis whites.[218]

Substantial survey data also indicates that black youth values regarding education are hardly different from white youth values, and are sometimes even more consistent with educational success. Studies have found, for instance, that black youth value doing well in school every bit as much as whites and often place an even greater emphasis on academic success than whites, despite the barriers they face to equal opportunity. Black tenth graders, for example, are much more likely than their white counterparts to discuss grades with their parents and to report that school is important to their peers. They are also more likely than similar whites to say that attending class regularly is important to their friends, that studying is important to their friends, and that getting good grades is important to their friends.[219]

Although many in the post-racial liberal camp, including President Obama, have made reference to the supposed tendency for black youth to deride other blacks who do well in school for "acting white," this slander upon the educational aspirations of black students bears little relationship to the real world of African American young people. Actual research—as opposed to the anecdotal reports of individual teachers or talking heads—has found that black students suffer no greater peer-based social penalty for doing well in school than students who are white.[220] Although black and Latino/a students have been found to often reject certain dress, music and speech styles as "acting white," they are no less likely than whites to value behaviors conducive to educational success,[221] such as studying or maintaining regular attendance.

One study from the Minority Student Achievement Network examined 40,000 students in grades seven through eleven and found no evidence that black students placed less value on education than their white peers. Black males were found to actually place *greater* emphasis on getting good grades than whites or Asians; in fact, white males were the *least* likely to say good grades were "very important" to them.[222] According to an examination of longitudinal data by sociologist Judith Blau of the University of North Carolina, low-income blacks are far more likely than low-income whites to discuss grades with parents, to say getting an education past high school is important to them, and to say that studying and good grades are important to their peer group. Furthermore, among students generally, blacks and Latino/as are less likely than whites to believe it is acceptable to be late for school, to skip classes, to copy someone else's homework or to talk back to teachers. In fact, high-income whites have the *lowest* scores on measures of academic ethics and integrity and are far more likely than low-income persons of color to endorse cheating and various forms of corner cutting to get ahead in school.[223] In other words, suggesting that blacks place inadequate emphasis on schooling, and less of an emphasis than whites—a key argument within both conservative and post-racial liberal analysis—is demonstrably false.

As for so-called welfare dependence, though rates of public assistance are higher in communities of color than in white communities—as would be expected, since persons of color are disproportionately poor and thus more able to qualify for assistance—it is untrue that welfare receipt, let alone dependence, is a normative behavior for people of color. For instance, at any given moment, 86 percent of blacks and 92 percent of Latinos are receiving no cash welfare assistance, only one in eight blacks are receiving any form of housing assistance, and prior to the latest economic downturn (which has forced many millions of all races to turn to nutritional assistance), only one in six were receiving food stamps. Among Latinos, only about one in twelve are receiving cash, one in twenty receive housing assistance, and only one in eight were receiving food stamps before the recent downturn.[224]

Furthermore, when comparing only white and black poor folks of truly comparable economic condition—since, after all, there are varying degrees of poverty and deprivation, and different degrees to which the poor possess certain assets or reserve resources upon which to draw in a crisis—the black poor are actually *less likely* to receive public assistance than the white poor.[225] And contrary to claims that persons receiving welfare (especially African Americans) receive assistance intergenerationally, two-thirds of women who received assistance as children will never receive aid as adults.[226] Likewise, 81 percent of those whose mothers received assistance will never themselves receive a penny of so-called welfare money once they become parents.[227]

So while the discussion about anti-poverty policy is an important one—and decent people can obviously disagree on the proper response to poverty—it is simply not the case that racial disparities between whites and people of color are principally due to cultural factors associated with poverty itself. Racial disparities manifest even when only comparing whites, blacks and Latino/as of similar class status and family composition. And for some disparities, like those that manifest in terms of health, the disparities are greatest at the *upper* end of the economic spectrum. Taken together, this is simply another reason why post-racial liberalism, with its rhetoric of racial transcendence and public policy agenda of colorblind universalism is inadequate for remedying racial divisions in America.

HOW COLORBLINDNESS CAN MAKE RACISM WORSE

Often those who advocate the policy agenda of colorblind universalism employ the metaphor of a "rising tide lifting all boats." President Obama himself, as mentioned earlier, used this imagery when asked if he had any plans to address the particular difficulties being faced by African Americans in the midst of the current economic crisis. Indeed, he had previously made the same argument in his book *The Audacity of Hope*. The position holds that if the economy is growing and adequate investments are being made in education and job training, all will benefit. Indeed, according to the proponents of this view, those at the bottom will benefit disproportionately, since, having so much more to gain from public investments, they will reap the lion's share of the rewards.

While there is certainly some truth to this view—for instance, there is no doubt that economic growth in the post–World War II era and throughout the 1960s boosted the economic profile of most all Americans, including those of color—it is also a troubling metaphor. After all, boats do not merely rise and ebb with the tide, in a vertical fashion. Boats also move horizontally. And when boats are locked in a race—as people in the United States are, for jobs, education, housing, etc.—the relative position of the boats is every bit as important as the mere fact of floating.

Furthermore, the rising tide metaphor is horribly simplistic. As with post–World War II economic growth, for instance, so too was the civil rights struggle important for opening the doors of opportunity to previously excluded people of color. Neither growth nor the movement alone would have likely produced the combined benefits that the two brought forward together. In fact, from the 1940s until the early to mid 1960s—during which time "universal" policies were implemented that largely ignored issues of racial discrimination and the impacts of bias on people of color—gaps in income between whites and blacks actually *increased*.[228] It was only after civil rights activism and race-conscious liberalism led to the inclusion of African Americans in previously whites-only, class-based efforts that those gaps began to narrow. This trend would then continue throughout the first few years of the 1970s,

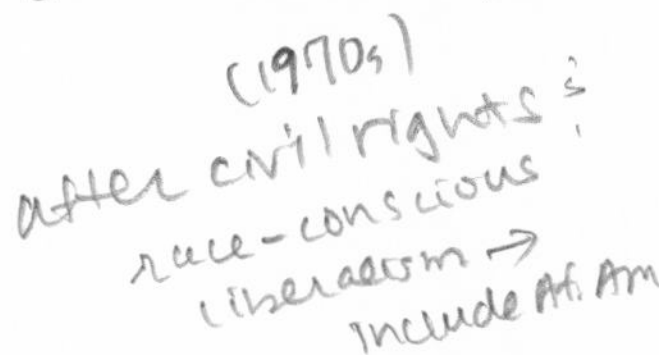

especially as affirmative action programs began to break down certain barriers in skilled trades and in management and professional positions.

More recent economic growth has been a bit different, though. Although the 1990s boom did "lift all boats" to an extent (in that, for instance, black poverty rates fell from 32 to 23 percent and black unemployment dropped significantly), the gaps between whites and blacks in terms of poverty, unemployment, net worth and other categories barely budged.[229] Indeed, in terms of wealth and assets, the gap increased, simply because whites, having started out with so much more of it, were able to transfer more of it to their children. And wealth, unlike income, tends to grow exponentially. Thus, in the 1990s when both whites and blacks were witnessing growing net worth and wealth, racial gaps continued to grow by over $16,000, on average, between the typical white and typical black family.[230] So yes, blacks were doing better than they had been, but whites were too, and the relative gains of whites tended to keep pace with, if not surpass, the relative gains made by people of color.

But even in light of such facts, perhaps there are those who would say, so what? Perhaps they would think it sufficient that everyone is doing better from year to year and generation to generation. To such persons, racial gaps don't matter, so long as everyone has enough to provide for themselves and their families. They might even suggest that to focus on the question of who has more than someone else is an exercise in futility, or even class envy.

But in fact, racial gaps matter, and for reasons that shouldn't be particularly difficult to understand. First, there is the issue of fairness itself. For whites to have such a relative advantage over people of color, and in such large measure because of the inertia carried over from past unequal opportunity, as well as ongoing discrimination, is unjust. These advantages are not earned, and thus to benefit from them is ethically dubious. Even more, those head starts allow whites to have advantages in multiple arenas of life, from jobs to education to housing, that will continue to place future generations of color at a disadvantage. In other words, the relative positions of whites and those of color will too often be transmitted across generational lines, having little to do with personal merit, hard work or effort.

Second, to the extent racial gaps persist—even if people of color do better from year to year thanks to universal policies of uplift—persons of color will continue to be priced out of the market for better housing and schools. So, for instance, as the society becomes wealthier, prices for things from college to health care to housing will increase. But if whites are gaining as much as (or more than) people of color—since all boats, after all, are rising—persons of color will be largely blocked from acquiring or gaining access to those more valuable assets. People of color will have more money, but whites will have that much more, and still be able to access goods and opportunities off-limits to everyone else. Even though people of color may be better off than their parents, their ability to truly compete with whites will remain stunted unless racial gaps themselves are narrowed.

Third, if racial gaps in well-being remain, racist thinking may actually be reinforced or made worse. For instance, if we say that race is of declining significance and that universal policies of uplift can reduce whatever disparities remain, but at the end of the day serious inequities persist (given the race-specific injuries that colorblind universalism cannot address), it will become almost *rational* to adopt racist views to explain those gaps. Such a conclusion would fit perfectly with the notion of meritocracy that is already quite prevalent in the culture, after all. Since racism is by definition about relative thinking—i.e., that members of group *x* are superior to group *y*—and given the embrace of meritocracy (the idea that anyone can make it if they try hard enough and that success results from superior talent), it shouldn't be surprising that persons confronted by racial disparities in income, housing, health and assets might conclude there were inherent reasons of superiority and inferiority that explain the relative positions of those different groups. This already happens far too often, which is why a book like *The Bell Curve*—which argues that blacks are biologically and genetically given to less intelligence than whites and Asians—could become a best-seller in the mid-1990s. But such thinking could become even more widespread were the politics of post-racial liberalism to succeed in shutting down conversation about ongoing racial discrimination and racism. Deprived of the critical context needed to understand the disparities we see, it would be all too easy for us to then embrace the individualistic and meritocratic narrative with which virtually all Americans were raised. Were we to do so, however, the consequences could be tragic—an actual intensification of racist thinking as a result of colorblindness: the ultimate irony.

Yet it is not only in the realm of racist thinking that colorblind universalism may present a problem. So too, the success of the post-racial narrative and colorblind policy making could reinforce institutional and structural racial inequities. After all, if the rhetoric of racial transcendence, which has been so instrumental to the political success of President Obama, manages to convince enough individuals of the need for colorblindness in public life, might it not also encourage colorblindness in the private realm? And by that I mean on the part of businesses, schools, doctors and others? And might not that colorblindness, by encouraging teachers, physicians, employers and others to ignore or downplay race, actually result in their ill-serving the needs of people who are confronted by racism, thereby actually helping to replicate it?

So, for instance, consider employers. Although for many years businesses have been engaged in efforts to enhance workplace diversity and equity—some doing far better than others, to be sure—if the logic of post-racial policy and colorblindness were to become increasingly popularized, it is conceivable that employers may abandon such efforts, sacrificing them on the altar of racial transcendence. No more deliberate efforts to recruit qualified people of color who may otherwise be overlooked. No more consideration of how the racialized opportunity structure—which under colorblindness is hardly recognized at all—may have shaped the formal résumés of job applicants, and yet not really tell an employer all they need to know about an applicant's abilities. Under a paradigm of colorblindness, employers would be encouraged to take résumés at face value, to ignore the role of old boys' networks in the procurement of so many jobs—and especially to ignore those networks' racial dynamic—and to act as though race doesn't matter, even as it will have impacted the experiences of the people applying for work with the particular employer, and those who ultimately come to work there.

Likewise teachers. If teachers are encouraged to downplay the role of racism in society and to be "colorblind" vis-à-vis their students, there is little doubt that they will underserve those students' needs. Research has found that black students are about 50 percent more likely than white students to say that teacher encouragement is critical to them, and a key determiner of how hard they work in school.[231] The reason for such a phenomena is not particularly difficult to discern. After all, black students are contending with any number of messages, from media and occasionally from educators, that they are less capable and not as smart. So for students experiencing so much *discouragement*—unlike whites who are typically perceived in far better terms and receive multiply reinforcing positive messages about their aptitude and ability—to have teachers express a belief in their abilities becomes a critical shot in the arm and incentivizes hard work. Yet if teachers operate on the basis of a colorblind mentality—one that says they shouldn't think about race, or the different impacts of race on their students—those teachers will likely not think to act on the basis of what this research tells us. They will likely teach without a conscious commitment to providing positive feedback, because the dominant group (of which they themselves will most often be a part) is not in need of encouragement in the same way.

Additionally, a colorblind mentality, taken to its logical conclusion in schools, would mean that educators would take little account of whether their curriculum was multicultural and inclusive of multiple voices and perspectives. To be colorblind, after all, is to not think about such things. Worse, colorblindness can also cause those who raise such matters, in violation of colorblind normalcy, to be accused of injecting race into arenas where it doesn't belong, and of violating a commitment to so-called universalism. Several years ago, when San Francisco public schools were discussing revising their literature curricula, this very thing happened: White parents, upset at the thought of replacing some of "the classics" with literature by authors of color—and ignoring that classics only became classics because certain people, almost all of them white, decided that they were the best writing—argued that the work of non-whites, while perhaps good literature, would be "too narrow" in its themes and wouldn't speak to the "universal" condition in the same way as, say, a fourteenth-century European like Geoffrey Chaucer. Colorblindness would only make this kind of thinking more common, resulting in schools that were less willing than ever to engage a critical analysis about what they teach and how they teach it.

Colorblindness would also reduce the likelihood of addressing racial disparities in discipline or tracking, not because these practices would suddenly vanish, but because we would be discouraged from keeping track of such troublesome information, or thinking about it at all. Validating colorblind thinking would make it more difficult to raise the issues, present the data and call for policy changes, since doing so would require profound color-consciousness and a willingness to utterly reject the rhetoric of racial transcendence.

Or consider physicians. Already the evidence, as presented above, suggests that doctors, despite their best intentions, too often dispense unequal care to their patients based on race. Oftentimes, this is the result of implicit racial biases. Recent research is beginning to show us the impacts of these disparities and the importance of taking race into consideration in the clinical setting so as to properly respond to the needs of patients of color. If black and brown patients are presenting symptoms that are in part the result of racialized stresses accumulated over time, a responsive physician will need to understand that truth, consider that factor and be trained on how to address issues of race and racism with patients. In short, they will need to see racism and discrimination as public health issues. But under a mentality of colorblindness, they will easily retreat back into the formalized and formulaic training that looks merely at symptoms themselves, and assumes that the causes of those symptoms are the same for everyone. For health professionals to be colorblind and look past race and racism will be to maintain or even deepen the existing injustice perpetrated against persons of color in terms of health.

TALKING CLASS, HEARING RACE: WHY POST-RACIAL LIBERALISM FAILS ON ITS OWN TERMS

But despite the evidence that race-based subordination and prejudice continue, that universal colorblindness cannot adequately address them, and that post-racial approaches could possibly make racism worse, proponents of the new paradigm have a ready fall-back position. Namely, they suggest that however imperfect a colorblind stance may be, it is the only politically viable path for progressive social policy. Even if colorblind universalism is inadequate as a tool for eradicating racial injustice, and even if the rhetoric of racial transcendence is dishonest, political reality is such that most whites simply will not get behind any remotely progressive policy regarding jobs, education or health care without a race-neutral approach, and so long as they believe such efforts are really about achieving racial equity. Those who subscribe to this view believe that we must, in effect, hide our commitment to racial justice behind a patina of universalism. At least by doing so, the advocates of post-racial liberalism hope, the society can make *some* progress toward social justice, even if imperfect and incomplete. In other words, it's better than nothing.

Putting aside the cynicism of such an approach, this argument—the ultimate *realpolitik* defense of post-racial liberalism—is rooted in assumptions that, upon careful examination, are unsupported and even contradicted by the evidence. In short, post-racial liberalism fails on its own terms.

The Racialization of Social Policy

There are several reasons why colorblind policy, at this point in time, cannot garner the political support for universal and progressive programs of uplift, which it claims to be able to deliver. First and foremost is the simple reality that the public, and particularly the white public, already views government spending on behalf of the have-nots or have-lessers, in racialized terms. In other words, post-racial liberals like President Obama may *say* that they are advocating colorblind universal programs to help all in need, but most white Americans apparently *hear* something else altogether. And once whites perceive that these universal efforts are really about racial redistribution, their opposition skyrockets. While there are certainly non-racial reasons that individuals may oppose efforts aimed at benefiting those at the bottom of the economic hierarchy—be they specified as people of color or not—research has found that there is a significant correlation between anti-black prejudice and such opposition.[232]

Studies confirm that perceptions of black laziness are central to white attitudes about spending on social programs and the extent to which such efforts are likely to be supported or rejected.[233] One comprehensive study of public assistance spending in the United States found that hostility to programs aimed at helping those in need is largely due to white racial resentment, specifically, the belief that persons of color will be the ones to benefit from said spending. Indeed, the study found that racial hostility to people of color, who are perceived as taking advantage of such programs, is more important to public opposition to these efforts than any other economic or political variable.[234] In other words, white perceptions about who the beneficiaries of social spending will be, impact the extent to which they are willing to get behind those efforts.

Apparently, the tendency for whites to hear race, and specifically "black people," when in fact neither race nor black people have even been mentioned, is quite common. In the case of any number of issues only tangentially related to race, the mere raising of said issues prompts white racial bias and triggers apparent implicit prejudices. As UCLA law professor Gary Blasi explains:

> The basic research on stereotyping suggests . . . any debate about placing restrictions on song lyrics will be affected by the indirect connection to race through rap music. Any reference to an urban issue, including such apparently neutral issues as parks or mass transit, will be affected by the underlying association of "urban" to "minority." Indeed, research suggests that race may be doing the most work in those public policy arenas where it has not been explicitly mentioned.[235]

These findings have profound implications for colorblind public policy efforts and those supporting such efforts. If public policies with even a remote connection to racial issues are likely to be viewed through a racial lens anyway, then the ability of colorblind efforts and the rhetoric of racial transcendence to effectively finesse white racial antipathy, or circumvent it in the interest of progressive social policy, is likely to be compromised. Given this reality, proposing so-called universal efforts to provide jobs, health care, better education and better housing opportunities for those without them, though it may be done in a "race-neutral" policy frame, may still prompt visions of racial others in the minds of the white public, thereby rendering the benefits of colorblindness moot. This isn't to say that such policies should not be supported, attempted and ultimately implemented. It is merely to say that they should not serve as an alternative to addressing racial inequity specifically. If the white public perceives any social program effort as racially coded anyway, better to raise the issues outright, rather than to be viewed as engaging in subterfuge to cover up some secretive racial redistribution scheme.

In fact, research has found that white racial resentment is likely to be activated in policy discussions *only* when it is allowed to remain sublimated and implicit. In other words, whites are primed to think in racialized terms—and negatively about blacks—only when the racial element of a policy consideration is subtle. When it is made explicit, whites do not act on their racial resentments as often, because to do so would conflict with their self-professed and stated commitments to fairness. As University of Texas professor Ismail White explains:

> Mendelberg (2001) argues that racial priming works because the racial cues present in these messages make racial schema (in this case, whites' attitudes about African Americans) more accessible in memory. Those schema are then used automatically in subsequent evaluations of candidates or policy issues. What makes Mendelberg's theory of racial priming unique, however, is her contention that, to have any impact on opinion, racial priming *must* function at an implicit level. At work . . . is a conflict for white Americans between their belief in the norm of equality on the one hand and their resentment toward blacks on the other. Awareness of the racial nature of a message, she argues, will lead most whites to reject that message because they would not want to violate the equality norm.[236]

For our purposes, this means that the Obama administration and others who claim to support progressive social policy should *not* shrink from discussing race, racism and racial inequity. If anything, they should talk about it more, and drag implicit racial biases that animate much opposition to those efforts into the light of day. Only in this manner can the contradiction between professed ideals and implicit biases be made salient. And only by exposing that contradiction can we hope to beat back reactionary priming of white racial resentment in public policy discussions.

The Messenger Matters: Seeing Obama as an Agent of Racial Redistribution

With regard to President Obama's agenda on health care, for example, there is evidence that many whites may perceive his efforts in racialized terms, no matter how universal the rhetoric with which he has tried to sell them, and no matter that he has specifically eschewed any discussion of, or focus on, racial disparity in health care per se. This could even be due to his rhetorical use of the term "public option" to describe the part of the reform initiative that would fall to the government. After all, use of the term "public" conjures images of other public amenities, like public transportation or public housing, both of which are so often seen as urban or "inner city" institutions utilized by people of color.

So, according to polling data from late 2008, whites with above-average levels of racial resentment toward blacks were less than half as likely as those with below-average resentment to support health care reform. Fewer than one in five whites for whom high prejudice and racial resentment manifested in the surveys supported reforming the nation's health care system; this, as opposed to about half of whites in the low-prejudice, low-resentment group who supported reform. Interestingly, these correlations between racial resentment and opposition to health care reform did not exist during the Clinton administration's attempts to reform health care, suggesting that there is something about the presence of Obama himself, as a man of color, that pushes racial buttons for large numbers of whites.[237]

In keeping with that notion, another study has found that a high level of racial bias against blacks is directly correlated with opposition to President Obama's health care proposals, boosting opposition among whites by about a third relative to those with low prejudice. Those with high levels of racial bias were just as likely as those with low bias to support Obama's proposals for reform *if they were presented as Bill Clinton's plan*, but when whites were told the proposal in front of them was Obama's, only whites with high levels of prejudice registered a drop in support, from 65 percent in favor, down to a mere 41 percent![238]

The question then, for proponents of colorblind universalism is this: if the white public, due to years of conditioning, perceives race-neutral public policy in race-specific terms—as some form of racial handout, and thus as something to be opposed—what is the political benefit to be derived from sticking with the rhetoric and policy agenda of post-racial liberalism? If the political upside of such a strategy is questionable, because of white racial resentment and implicit bias, then what reasons remain for finessing issues as important as racial inequity and discrimination? Might it not be better to call those things out directly, challenge white racial conditioning, and make the closing of racial gaps a national mission, in keeping with the very philosophical tradition to which the president so often appealed in his campaign? Might it not be better to explain why racial inequity needs to be addressed, as both a moral and practical national imperative? Furthermore, given the research on racial priming and white racial resentment—which indicates that only when race is allowed to remain implicit does priming it succeed[239]—might it not be strategically wiser to explicitly call out the racial aspects of opposition to health care reform and other progressive initiatives?

If whites are already thinking in racialized terms, why not seek to steer that cognitive process in a constructive direction, rather than allowing it to fester unmolested thanks to a strategic silence, which, in the end, isn't really all that strategic?

Post-Racialism as Unilateral Disarmament in the Face of Right-Wing Attacks

The need for this constructive steering is especially apparent, given the way in which the political opponents of progressive social policy seem committed to capitalizing on white resentment in order to torpedo any efforts to reduce inequities, be they racial or economic. Knowing how the public often perceives spending on social programs—having effectively played on white hostility to such efforts all throughout the 1980s and 1990s—conservatives have consistently injected racial symbolism and linguistic memes into the political conversation about President Obama and his policy agenda.

Glenn Beck, as previously noted, has repeatedly suggested that President Obama's push for health care reform is really about obtaining reparations for blacks. That he would make such a claim even when Obama's plan has never included *any* specific policies for addressing racial inequity, and even when he has repeatedly avoided even discussing, let alone trying to solve those disparities, indicates the extent to which conservatives are prepared to deploy race and racial resentment against the president.[240] Beyond commentators like Beck, more "respectable" outlets for conservatism have also played the racial resentment card against the president. So, for instance, an editorial in *Investor's Business Daily* referred to health care reform as "affirmative action on steroids" and also suggested that it amounted to a form of racial reparations for slavery.[241]

Indeed, the amount of blatantly race-based invective aimed at Obama since his inauguration has been extraordinary. Consider Rush Limbaugh, who in the midst of a recent diatribe against the president, threw in a complaint that among the nation's biggest problems is that we're "so multicultured and fractured." Not divided by racism and prejudice of course, but by multiculturalism itself, and presumably the failure of all groups to accept dominant white cultural narratives and norms.[242] Three days later, in keeping with this theme, Limbaugh lambasted the left (of which he presumes the president to be a chief resident, naturally), for "celebrating diversity" and thereby endangering a "distinct American culture."[243]

Elsewhere, discussing the nomination of Sonia Sotomayor to the Supreme Court, Limbaugh said, "They [minorities] want to use their power as a means of retribution. That's what Obama is all about."[244] In a long rant about the nomination, in which he lamented the supposed timidity of the Republican Party in the face of what Limbaugh perceives as an all-out racial assault against whites, he went even further:

> How do you get promoted in the Barack Obama administration? By hating white people . . . make white people the new oppressed minority . . . and they're [the Republican Party] going right along with it 'cuz they're shutting up, moving to the back of the bus. They're saying "I can't use that drinking fountain, OK! I can't use that restroom, OK!"[245]

Discussing the arrest of African American scholar Henry Louis Gates in Cambridge, Massachusetts (and Obama's mild criticism of the officer who arrested him after Gates became angry at the insinuation that he might have been breaking into his own home), Limbaugh bellowed that "white policemen are under assault" by the president,[246] and that "here you have a black president trying to destroy a white policeman."[247] In response to the same incident—in which the president suggested the Cambridge police acted "stupidly" in arresting Gates (a true statement given the law in Massachusetts, under which Gates had *not* been guilty of the crime for which he was arrested)[248]—Beck claimed that Obama's comment proved the president was a "racist" who "has a deep-seated hatred for white people or white culture."[249]

To Limbaugh too, Obama's anti-white animus extends much further than merely to white law enforcement officers. Thus, his September 15, 2009, rant in which he all but blamed President Obama for a fight on a school bus in Illinois, in which two black students attacked a white student. Although police determined the incident had *nothing* to do with race or racial animus between the attackers and the victim, Limbaugh told his listeners, "In Obama's America, the white kids now get beat up with the black kids cheering."[250]

Throughout the summer, during some of the most intense commentary on proposed health care reform, Limbaugh elevated his racial resentment and fear-mongering to new heights, consistently pushing comparisons between president Obama and Adolf Hitler, as if to suggest that Obama was a racially driven, perhaps even totalitarian leader. To wit, his remarks that the "Obama health care logo is damn close to a Nazi swastika logo," and that "Adolf Hitler, like Barack Obama, ruled by dictate,"[251] or to the effect that there are several "similarities between the Democrat Party of today and the Nazi Party in Germany."[252] The Hitler/Nazi meme was also advanced by Glenn Beck, who said in April 2009 that the country today reminds him of "the early days of Adolf Hitler."[253]

Additionally, Limbaugh has insisted that Obama's "entire economic program is reparations"[254]—seconding Beck's claims regarding the president's health care plan—and that Obama "is more African in his roots than he is American," and is "behaving like an African colonial despot."[255] Meanwhile, one of the main figures in the conservative and libertarian "Tea Party" movement, Mark Williams, referred to the president on his blog as an "Indonesian Muslim turned welfare thug."[256]

Sadly, these race-based attacks against the president are all too common, even among the general public. Thus, one can read references to Obama's daughter Malia, posted on the popular conservative Web site *Free Republic*, as "ghetto trash," "street trash" and a "typical street whore"—posts to which almost no one on the site objected in the least.[257] Or consider the post on the Facebook page of Young Republican leader Audra Shay—which Shay herself laughed about at the time—in which one of Shay's friends, Eric Pike, wrote, "Obama Bin Lauden is the new terrorist. . . . Muslim is on there side . . . need to take this country back from all of these mad coons . . . and illegals."[258]

Elsewhere, Republican and conservative activists have likened Michelle Obama to an ape,[259] distributed e-mails condemning "Obamacare" that picture the president dressed as a witch doctor with a bone through his nose,[260] and appeared at rallies with signs suggesting health care reform will take money from senior citizens to give care to undocumented Mexicans.[261] Other prominent signs at these rallies have announced that Obama intends to put white people in slavery[262] or have pictured the president with a Hitler mustache. Still others have featured swastikas and called into question the president's nationality, most insisting he is a Kenyan or, as one sign put it, a "Lyin' African."[263] At another rally, white audience members cheered when a white man assaulted a black woman and ripped up her poster of Rosa Parks.[264]

That right-wing leaders are so willing to deploy—and the public so willing to accept—racist rhetoric and other invective aimed at stoking white resentment and fear, even against a president who almost never discusses race at all, suggests the likely inadequacy of post-racialism as a paradigm for fighting racial inequities. The rhetoric of racial transcendence so critical to advocates of post-racial liberalism—which has already been shown to rest on a foundation of untruth, given the reality of persistent racism—cannot possibly drown out the hateful and often unhinged rantings of those insistent on painting the president as an anti-white bigot. Likewise, the policy agenda of colorblind universalism—which despite its race neutrality is still seen by so many as a veiled attempt at racial redistribution—will not likely gain sufficient political support for it to be successful, even on its own terms (those of political expedience), to say nothing of being successful at reducing the racial disparities against which it is being deployed.

Unfortunately, the president's refusal to fight back against these tactics—and he has studiously denied *any* racial motivation for even the most blatantly racial attacks to which he has been subjected—appears unlikely to alter the trajectory of reactionary tactics and rhetoric. Obama has, again and again, sought to be as racially unthreatening as possible to white Americans, distancing himself from his Attorney General when the latter noted that the United States had often been a "nation of cowards" when it came to discussing race,[265] backtracking on his criticism of the Cambridge police after they arrested Harvard professor Henry Louis

Gates[266]—and this, again, even though his comment had been accurate, given the law in that state—and disagreeing with former president Carter when the latter suggested that *some* of the attacks against President Obama were rooted in white racial antipathy toward him as a black man.[267] Despite Obama's aversion to even discussing race, white conservatives have consistently deployed the rhetoric of white resentment against him.

To refuse to fight back, far from disarming these forces of bigotry or depriving them of a point of attack, has done nothing to blunt their efforts. Indeed, it may have emboldened them. It may, in the end, amount to little more than unilateral disarmament. Rather than responding to white fear-mongering with straight talk and challenging white Americans to live up to the creed they claim to embrace, Obama and others in the camp of post-racial liberalism seem content to "take the high road." What they fail to realize, sadly, is that the road they walk leads nowhere. It will not lead to political success, and it will not reduce racial disparities in any walk of national life. It is not a workable paradigm for thought or action. It needs to be abandoned.

THREE

Illuminated Individualism: A Paradigm for Progressive Color-Consciousness

Of course, it is not sufficient to call for the abandonment of one paradigm—colorblindness, or post-racial liberalism more broadly—without advocating a better alternative. To diagnose the shortcomings of one school of thought without at least beginning to lay out the contours of something that might replace it would seem to suggest that there were no ways to alter the course upon which the nation is currently headed. But in truth, we do have choices to make, and make them we must.

So now let us turn toward a different path, one that can offer alternative ways of operating, institutionally and personally, and which if we choose to walk it, may yet help move the nation forward on the road to racial equity. That path I call *illuminated individualism.*

As we know, the United States has long been a nation that prides itself on its commitment to individualism. Individual rights and liberties are enshrined prominently in the Constitution and are meant to facilitate both personal and collective achievement. Though the nation practiced profound and formalized hypocrisy with regard to those values for most of its history, thanks to institutionalized white supremacy, the values themselves have been part of the national narrative from the beginning. Much of that focus on individuality has proved beneficial; for instance, it makes us quick to raise the banner of liberty whenever we see it threatened—and so, in that regard, Americans demonstrate a strong libertarian streak to guard against encroachment upon our freedoms. But other aspects of the individualism ethic can be troubling, among them the tendency to place personal success and profit-making above the well-being of the society and the natural environment, hyper-competitiveness—which, though it may lead to great societal wealth, also tends to create significant inequalities and encourage materialism among those living in such a culture—and a kind of "me-first" mentality, which can quickly take on the characteristics of collective narcissism.

In an attempt to blunt some of the more isolating aspects of individualism, liberals often emphasize the notion of the collective good, or the good of the community. In traditional leftist configurations, the collective good is most often articulated in class-conscious terms: workers collectively organizing for their interests in the face of economic exploitation by capitalist owners of production. In recent liberal terms—and especially in the realm of post-racial liberalism—that collective interest has been conceived of in national terms. It is represented by Jim Sleeper's admonition in his book *Liberal Racism* that "liberals should be working overtime to identify and nurture at least a few shared national principles and bonds that deepen a sense of common belonging and nourish democratic dispositions."[268] It is articulated in President Obama's claim about the nation being one "United States of America," not merely in name but in fact, rather than a nation deeply divided along lines of race. So too with his recent comment to the effect that he thinks it a "mistake to start thinking in terms of particular ethnic segments of the United States rather than to think that we are all in this together."[269]

But in the case of both conservative individualism and liberal Americanism, the real effects of racial identity, class status, gender, sexual orientation, resident status and several other categories are overlooked. Both liberals and conservatives appear committed to an understanding of self largely divorced from the diversity of communities and identities that shape us, from our likely family histories to our cultural norms and traditions, to the experiences we will have, and thus to the perspectives we are likely to develop.

It's not that our individual identities or national identity are unimportant: They too have meaning. But they are both mediated and moderated by our other identities, as whites or people of color, men or women, rich or poor, right on down the line. To act as though our individual identities or mere identities as Americans are sufficient to capture a sense of who we are is absurd. Surely to be a gay, lesbian, bisexual or transgendered American is to experience everyday life quite differently, in terms of opportunity and experience, than one who is straight. To be a minimum wage–earning adult in the United States is to live an American life extraordinarily unlike that lived by a millionaire. To be a woman is to have individual experiences that cannot be conceived of by a man. So too, to be a person of color in a nation where color has meant something *from the beginning* cannot possibly be seen as conferring no unique experiences, insights or perspectives upon those who have lived under the designation. And by extension, to be *white* in a nation where whiteness has also meant something must suggest a life trajectory different in many ways from that of someone who is black, Latino, Asian, Arab or indigenous to the continent.

In short, we can't all "just be Americans," because we never have been just that. For whites, Americanism was something that could be taken for granted (indeed it was synonymous with their racial group), while for others it has never been something to which they could lay claim as readily. And we can't all "just be individuals," because *no one* is just that, nor has anyone ever lived as such, anywhere, at any time, on the face of the Earth. Indeed, there is no such thing as an individual human being abstracted from their social context. Human beings have never lived in isolation. Humans have always been social, and have experienced life as members of certain groups, be they tribes, communities, families and in more modern times nationalities, races, economic classes and religions. To speak of the individual as if their various group identities did not exist—or at least, not to any degree that matters—is to speak of an abstraction: a word with a dictionary meaning but no encyclopedic one.

ILLUMINATED INDIVIDUALISM AS A KEY TO FAIRNESS AND EQUITY

Illuminated individualism tries to recognize this truth: that we are made up of many identities, and that these matter. Although it is a paradigm for thought and action that absolutely recognizes the value of the individual and seeks to treat each person as the unique being they are, it also rests on a recognition that a person's position in various groups will have affected their experiences, and thus their perceptions of life. In order to treat them as the unique persons they *truly* are, as opposed to an abstraction, our institutions, our public policies and all of us on a personal level must resolve to take account of those factors that shape others, and ourselves. When it comes to race, we must be color-conscious, not colorblind.

Individualism needs illumination, much as a room needs illumination so that we may see those inside more clearly. If you've ever entered a dimly lit room when someone was inside, you probably were able to sense, perhaps instinctively, that there was someone there. But until the lights were turned on, you were likely unable to make that person out, to tell who they were, to process any important, defining information about them. The same is true about individualism, abstracted from group identities. If we don't examine the latter, we won't really see the former clearly.

Beyond the merely philosophical, what does all this mean? It means that we must resolve to consider race and the impact of racial identity on the lives of others and on ourselves. We must weave into our personal thinking and our institutional settings practices, procedures and policies that take account of race and its meaning, and in recognition of that meaning, resolve to do everything possible to minimize the likelihood of discriminatory treatment. Only by having open and honest conversations about race and racism, and our own internalized preconceptions, can we hope to keep implicit biases at bay and create real equity of opportunity. While there are many who care little about these issues (and indeed, nearly half of whites polled in the late 1990s said that most within their group simply "don't care" whether or not blacks move forward in society),[270] post-racial adherents, almost by definition, do. This book was not written for those persons who are unconcerned about equity or openly hostile to it. It was written for those who passionately wish to see inequities eradicated, and are prepared to push forward an agenda to accomplish that. Although it is my contention that the post-racial approach fails to solve the problems of racial disparity, its inadequacy owes not to the lack of concern on the part of its proponents. Rather, it rests upon the faulty assumptions post-racial liberals make about the society in which we live. Where colorblindness will almost surely fail them—fail us—in its ability to achieve equity and fairness, perhaps illuminated individualism can succeed.

First, let us not underestimate the importance of adopting a new mindset. Some prefer direct policy prescriptions, and we will come to those shortly. But before getting there, let us understand how critical the color-conscious, race-conscious mindset alone can be for generating more equitable treatment of others. The good news is that there is much we can do, each of us, without having to wait for the state to act. Too often, progressives assume that only government action—a mandate of some sort—can realize the social conditions we seek. But in truth, if those who proclaim a commitment to racial justice and equity were to collectively move to implement color-conscious, racism-conscious policies and practices in our workplaces, schools and communities, we could begin the process of transformation, even if the state remains hostile to such efforts, and even if post-racial adherents continue to avoid the subject matter altogether.

First, we must acknowledge the ways in which we have been conditioned to have racially prejudiced beliefs, however implicit, and how—unless we take special care not to—we may fall prey to those biases, despite our best intentions, thereby perpetuating injustice. The recognition of this alone can help us begin to operate in a more equitable manner. Simply put, it is easier for individuals to confront—and thus perhaps defeat—racial biases once they are brought out into the open. Because stereotypes are controlled by what psychologists call "automatic processes," they are not subject to critical analysis and self-reflection the way one's actual beliefs are. Since personally held beliefs—which are governed by "controlled processes"—are the key to challenging stereotypes (and thus guarding against their activation), it can be helpful to drag one's biases into the light of conscious thought as a way to better prompt self-monitoring. As legal scholar Jody Armour explains:

> Research has demonstrated that low- and high-prejudiced people are equally prone to stereotype-congruent responses when they cannot consciously monitor their responses to questions. However, low- and high-prejudiced people have given very different responses when they have had to think consciously about what their responses imply about self-image.[271]

become aware of racial biases

In other words, research suggests that people need to be given opportunities to act on their better natures. But this, in turn, requires that they be confronted with the reality that, unbidden, they may have the tendency to do the opposite. Research on gender bias has further confirmed the importance of forcing us to confront the contradiction between our stated ideals and actual behavior. According to one study, when respondents were not prompted to think about gender identity in a given situation—and yet the opportunity was present to act in a gender-biased manner—the subjects tended to describe themselves and others in far more traditional and stereotypical gender terms. But when gender was made salient to their conversation, and thus the possibility of operating in a gender-biased fashion would be made more obvious, they inhibited the expression of stereotypes and their discussion took on far more egalitarian tendencies, in line with their expressed, conscious feelings. This would suggest that implicit biases can influence perceptions and behavior when they are allowed to remain sublimated, but can be challenged and neutralized so long as individuals are made to think about them in a way that allows them to check their own tendencies.

Perhaps the best example of this process was demonstrated over eighty years ago, in one of the nation's most famous criminal trials. In 1926, famed defense attorney Clarence Darrow came out of retirement to defend Dr. Ossian Sweet, his two brothers and several of his friends after they were accused of murder. Sweet and his co-defendants were being tried for shooting two white men (one of whom died from his wounds) after a mob of whites had gathered outside their Detroit home and begun pelting the house with rocks. The mob had hoped to run the Sweet family out of the otherwise all-white neighborhood into which they had just moved. After the first trial ended with a hung jury, Henry Sweet, Ossian's brother, was retried first. Knowing that the all-white jury was likely biased against his black clients (and for reasons explicitly owing to their own racism), Darrow began his closing statement—which is one of the most famous in legal history, and which lasted approximately eight hours—by calling out the jury members for their prejudices. He noted that had the trial been of a group of white men charged with killing a group of blacks who had been trying to attack them, they would likely be handing the defendants medals of honor, rather than considering punishment. By priming the jurors to think about race, and their own biases, Darrow could then challenge them to rise above their conditioning and to be fair, in spite of their passions and prejudices. It became a challenge to act in accordance with deeply held and positive values. And it worked. Henry Sweet was acquitted, and the charges against the others were ultimately dropped.[272]

Had Darrow chosen to avoid priming the racial frame in this instance, and rather opted for a colorblind, race-neutral approach, it is likely that the jurors would have found Sweet guilty. Their implicit biases, unexposed to the light of day, would have been harder for them to check. They would have been unable to confront the contradiction between their professed values and their internalized biases. It was only color-conscious and frankly *racism-conscious* lawyering by Darrow that made possible his clients' victory. As Armour explains:

> To control a bad habit, a person must first recall it consciously and then intentionally inhibit it as he or she responds in

> ways consistent with his or her personally endorsed beliefs or attitudes.[273]

Additional research on mock jury decisions confirms the value of raising matters of race explicitly, rather than allowing what are often deeply entrenched implicit biases to go unspoken and unmonitored. In one study, mock jurors were presented with a case involving a fight between two ballplayers—one black, one white—on the same team. When jurors were told that the defendant [who in some tests was the white player, and in others, the black player] had been the target of racial abuse from others on his team before assaulting his teammate, the jurors demonstrated no racial bias. They were equally likely to convict a white defendant as a black one, and appeared to take the racial abuse of the black player every bit as seriously as when the abuse was directed at the white player. But when the jurors were told only the respective races of the defendant and the victim—and were not told anything about racism having been directed at the defendant—jurors were almost 30 percent more likely to convict the black defendant than the white one.[274]

This research suggests that when race is made a salient issue in a deliberation—in other words, when whites are forced to think consciously about racism as a subject—they operate in a less biased manner than if such a frame remains unprimed. In their article "Race and Juries: An Experimental Psychology Perspective," Samuel Sommers and Omoniyi Adekanmbi provide further explication of this phenomenon:

> When thoughts about race are made salient during their review of a trial (such as, for example, when the incident in

question is racially charged) or when strong normative cues against the expression of racial bias are present (for example, when judicial instructions emphasize the importance of avoiding prejudice), white jurors will be motivated to correct for the perceived influence of a defendant's race and to render an objective, "color-blind" decision. However, in the absence of normative cues regarding race, even subtle racial biases are likely to make their way to the surface and to influence judgments.[275]

Although jury settings are not precisely the same as other real-world conditions, the internal psychological processes at work in such cases, which demonstrate the value of explicitly raising matters of race, apply in other settings as well. One can imagine, for instance, the value of directly raising concerns about potential racial bias in workplace hiring decisions, college admissions, policing and the provision of medical care among other contingencies. Trainings that educate persons in authority to take special care *not* to act on implicit bias seem to be, at a minimum, a way to reduce the likelihood of triggered racial bias and discrimination. In which case, yet again, we see that color-conscious, rather than colorblind efforts prove superior as a hedge against unfairness.

This is especially true when decision makers could easily latch on to non-racial reasons for making decisions that are, at root, about race after all. The research on implicit biases, for instance, indicates that such biases are most likely to be activated and acted upon in those cases where there is ambiguity as to the racial motivation for a given action.[276] So, for instance, in most employment settings, or when it comes to college admissions, or writing home loans, or policing, or teaching in an urban school, it would be easy to make decisions that were influenced by racial bias but could be rationalized as non-racial. For instance, an employer can always say—and technically be honest in saying it—that the applicant of color just "didn't fit in" for some unspecified reason. So too they could justify a decision not to hire an applicant of color for seemingly valid reasons: slightly less experience, less impressive prior references or vague factors of personality and so-called "soft skills" involving communication style. But if the employer's perceptions about those factors are themselves skewed by implicit biases—and research suggests that this is a distinct possibility—then the "race-neutral" process by which the applicant of color would then be denied the job would have been anything *but* fair.

Likewise, a teacher could over-discipline students of color because they truly perceive such students to be more disruptive, even though evidence indicates there is no racial difference between the rates at which whites and non-white students commit serious school-rule infractions. So too, a loan officer can find non-racial reasons for denying a black, Latino or Asian loan applicant a mortgage (or at least offering such a loan only at a higher interest rate)—such as blotches on the applicant's credit record—but this wouldn't justly insulate that officer from a charge of racial bias. After all, it may well be the case that the loan officer has overlooked or minimized the importance of similar blotches on the credit reports of whites because of internalized biases in favor of the dominant group, which work to the detriment of persons of color. In part, this kind of discrimination occurs because a person's internalized biases can cause them to *expect* certain traits in a person of color, such as bad creditworthiness, aggressiveness or lesser ability. Then, with such expectations in place, the mind will often process otherwise ambiguous information in a way that causes what a person sees to conform to their expectations.[277]

According to the available research, implicit biases are best confronted and countered by appeals to conscious, publicly held values and honest reflection on the unfortunate gaps that often exist between our aspirations and our achieved levels of equanimity. As Drew Westen, professor of psychology at Emory University, explains:

> The scientific data suggest two strategies that are, however, effective in addressing unconscious prejudices. . . . The first is to remind people of their conscious values, which tend to be our better angels on race. The average American strongly agrees with the sentiment that "In America, we don't discriminate against anybody because of their color, ethnicity or anything else"—whether they see that as a statement of actuality or aspiration. And they mean it—and will act on it, as long as their conscious values are active and guiding their behavior. The second is to speak directly to the conflict between those values and the attitudes we hold at some level that we wish we didn't. . . . It's about talking to people like grown-ups. . . . The best antidote to unconscious bias is self-reflection. And the best way to foster that self-reflection is through telling the truth.[278]

In short, it is only by taking away the ability of decision makers to content themselves with the assumption that their process has been fair—and this means by raising the specter of unfairness as a hedge against mistreatment—that we can hope to imbue our institutional practices with greater equanimity. To do otherwise—to remain silent about the chance of unjust treatment in the name of colorblindness, for instance—is to intensify the risk of discriminatory treatment. Patricia Devine puts it best when she notes, "nonprejudiced responses take intention, attention and effort." In other words, it is simply not enough to assume that people will act on the basis of fairness.[279] While our intentions may be good, subconscious processes are at work when it comes to issues like race, gender, class and other elements of identity and of our perception of others. Doing the right thing requires working at it, and making ourselves and others aware of the gap between professed beliefs and internalized biases can help produce more deliberative, empathic interactions.[280] Colorblindness, by virtue of keeping matters of racism and discrimination under wraps—and refusing to raise the subjects for fear of offending or sowing division—actually goes against every bit of modern research on how the brain processes racial stereotypes and can influence our behaviors in a way that causes us to act on them.

The importance of deliberately raising the specter of racial bias, as opposed to sublimating the subject in the name of colorblindness, is especially pertinent to the current debate over health care and other policy items on the president's agenda. While the Obama administration has sought to downplay the role of racism in the opposition to health care reform, this research may point to the value of raising such issues, if for no other reason than to serve as a check on that portion of the opposition that is motivated by implicit biases. If opponents of the president's agenda are allowed to avoid facing the possibility that their motivation is racial bias—and they can avoid this possibility more easily given the president's own unwillingness to raise the issue—they can continue to operate behind a veil of innocence and plausible deniability, never forced to confront the possible contradiction between their professed values and their internalized beliefs. Yet, if forced to address the potentially race-based motivations for their positions, it is possible that at least some may soften their opposition, if only to bring their actions in line with their professed ideals. At the very least, raising the issue will increase the costs to those opposed to progressive policy and force them to demonstrate their racial equanimity, rather than allowing their fair-mindedness to be taken as a given. As such, conservatives will have to discuss the issue on progressive grounds, rather than being allowed to define the terms of the debate, on health care or other issues.

Likewise, honesty about racism seems best suited to boosting support for progressive social policy, contrary to the claims of post-racial liberals. In studies conducted with college students, Philip Mazzocco of the Kirwan Institute at Ohio State University found that when whites are confronted with comprehensive information about ongoing racial disparities, the structural reasons for those disparities *and* a critique of the common belief in meritocracy, they are often willing to support progressive social policy aimed at producing racial equity. On the other hand, simply discussing racial disparities without the structural analysis and explanation for those disparities, or without a critique of the deeply internalized faith in America as a meritocracy, often backfires and causes greater opposition to such efforts. Without the discussion of institutional racism and ongoing mistreatment, and without being challenged as to their belief in meritocracy, many whites actually tend to blame people of color for the disparities they experience.

Such findings indicate the importance of honest and color-conscious discussions about racism and the inadequacy of color-blind approaches. To the extent that post-racial liberals openly admit racial disparities but then downplay the race-specific and even racist reasons for those disparities, they weaken the case for addressing them in the minds of whites. And to the extent that many post-racial liberals, President Obama first and foremost, continue to reinforce the idea of the United States as a meritocracy where "anyone can make it"—even a black guy named Barack Hussein Obama—they undermine the case for taking action on racial disparities, because they leave in place the idea that those at the bottom could better their own lives if only they tried harder. Based on his research, Mazzocco concludes:

> It is tempting to take a color-blind approach that reduces attention to race and instead refers to other categories, such as class. . . . However, recent advances within the fields of social psychology and sociology have demonstrated that the color-blind approach to race may be impractical, at best, and at worst harmful to the quest for racial equality and interracial good will. In contrast, a color-conscious approach is not only feasible, but has been proven to be an effective means of targeting race-related attitudes. Color-conscious approaches show promise in fostering an appreciation of another group's positive societal contributions, as well as structural constraints and advantages. . . .[281]

ILLUMINATED INDIVIDUALISM IN PRACTICE

Beyond merely resolving to be more aware of how race has shaped our lives, there is much that an individual can do in keeping with this color-conscious mindset. Significantly, most of the color-conscious actions we can take require no government mandate, funding or initiative at all. Though there are public policy recommendations for which we should push as well—and those will be examined shortly—conscientious individuals committed to promoting equity can resolve to practice illuminated individualism on their own, in workplaces, schools and other settings.

Raising Awareness of Race Early and Often

First and foremost, parents need to begin discussing race and racism with children far earlier than is commonly believed. While it is often thought that children are too "innocent" to notice race, to think about color or to ascribe any meaning to the differences they observe, literally *all* the recent research on child development suggests otherwise. Children at very young ages, well before school begins, are beginning to notice color, and indeed draw conclusions about what differences in color mean. Often, those conclusions are rooted in biased assumptions picked up from observing the larger society: from media imagery, from those they see (and don't see as often) in authority positions, noticing who lives (and doesn't live) in their neighborhoods, and other dynamics.[282]

New research suggests that babies as young as six months of age begin to judge others on the basis of skin color.[283] Although these early judgments are likely the normal reactions of children simply trying to categorize their worlds and make sense of difference—in which case they may initially make in-group/out-group judgments based on an obvious physical characteristic like color—unless parents mediate those judgments and discuss race and racism with their kids, the preconceptions can become normalized fairly quickly. Children, left to their own devices, will often conclude that racial others are less desirable. If their parents' social circles, their neighborhoods and their schools are largely racially homogenous (and for whites, if they can also see representation of other whites throughout prominent leadership roles in the society), it becomes reasonable to conclude that the explanation for people of color being absent from those circles, communities and schools is because there must be something *wrong* with them. Children, after all, are typically egocentric, in that they perceive their friends, their neighborhoods and their schools as "the best." If those friends, neighborhoods and schools lack racial and ethnic diversity, it becomes increasingly likely that they will decide those persons of color who are absent from these spaces are absent because they are not as good. Only by discussing the social factors like racism—past and present—that influence where people live (and don't), where they go to school (and don't) and who we know (and don't know, as well) can parents hope to arm their children with the information needed to critically process matters of racial difference and division. This calls for an inherently race-conscious approach.

The bad news is that such an approach is one that most white parents refuse to take, opting instead to simply avoid conversations about race, unwilling or unable to introduce the matter to their children. Indeed, according to research published in the *Journal of Marriage and Family*, parents of color are about three times as likely to discuss race with their kids as white parents are. In fact, three out of four white parents never, or nearly never, discuss race with their children.[284] Sometimes, white parents claim that avoiding the topic is intended to maintain their children's sense of innocence or fair play, and not to complicate their worlds with information about injustice. While this may be the motivation behind parental silence, evidence indicates that the worlds of children are already plenty complicated when it comes to thinking about race, and silence does nothing to make them less so.

The good news is that when white parents *do* take up the challenge and discuss these issues with their kids, the effort can have a dramatic effect, improving the racial attitudes of those children towards others, enhancing empathy and reducing implicit biases. But once again, to have this effect, a color-conscious, race-conscious and racism-conscious approach will be necessary. Much as parents of girls regularly seek to counter-program against gender stereotypes (and even conscientious parents of boys do this fairly regularly nowadays), so too must parents take an active role in countering racial stereotypes, which in turn requires that one must openly *discuss* those stereotypes first, so as to then debunk them and promote counter-stereotypical thinking.

Additionally, teaching about racial injustice and mistreatment of people of color—historically and still today—though it can prompt certain feelings of white guilt in the short run, can also help build empathy and understanding among white children. Failing to discuss that history leaves children unable to process the racial divisions that so often manifest in the present, from where people live to what kind of jobs they have to the schools they attend. The longer we take to discuss these matters with young people, the more likely they will come to assume that the divisions they see are "natural," or "just the way things are," or worse, the result of inherent and immutable racial differences between whites and people of color. Of course, it is important to not merely discuss injustice in a vacuum, or in a way that results in increased polarization between whites and students of color. Fortunately, if the material is taught accurately (which would mean, for instance, also discussing the white allies who have stood in solidarity with people of color in every era to fight racism), that guilt response can be diminished, while making the empathy and solidarity connection among white children stronger.[285]

Parents of color must also speak with their children about racism. Though such parents are often worried about frightening their children with information that might lead them to anticipate mistreatment, having at least occasional, preparatory conversations can be beneficial to their children's development. Research shows that children reared by parents who prepare them for racism and how to cope with it report less distress in response to mistreatment, if and when it occurs.[286] Recent research has discovered that children as young as third grade, and certainly by middle school (around the age of 10 or 11), are increasingly aware of the racial stereotypes commonly held against people of color in the larger society. And for students of color, their awareness of negative stereotypes about their own group can lead to increased anxiety in school, thereby driving down performance on tests and various measures of academic achievement.[287] Though this concept—known in the literature as "stereotype threat"—has long been known to affect young adults of color, the fact that studies now demonstrate its impact on young children indicates how important it is to have conversations processing and challenging those stereotypes early on. And when it comes to teaching about injustices committed against persons of color, so long as teachers and parents present the issue through a lens of resistance—in other words, discuss what the targets of oppression did in *response* to challenge injustice, rather than merely presenting the victimization narrative itself—there is reason to believe the lesson can be empowering rather than distressing.

Teaching young people to think and talk about issues of race can serve them well in later life, while failing to do so can actually contribute to unnecessary racial tension. For instance, research from Northwestern University has found that whites often avoid interracial contact, in large part out of a fear that they may say something or do something perceived as racist.[288] This fear of "messing up" is no doubt intensified by a lack of practice and comfort interacting across racial lines and discussing matters of race openly. Ironically, when people of color perceive that whites are avoiding mentioning or discussing race, additional research has found that this actually contributes to the belief that those whites are likely covering up racial prejudice. In other words, many whites avoid the issue out of a fear that they'll be perceived as racist, and it is the very avoidance of the issue that leads many people of color to think of them in *precisely* those terms.[289]

Color-Consciousness in Our Institutional Lives

Conscientious persons can also operate on the basis of illuminated individualism in their professional lives. And we can do this without waiting for the government to mandate it, indeed even if government leaders themselves remain stuck in a paradigm of colorblindness.

We can make race salient in the way we process employment applications, evaluate co-workers over whom we have supervisory responsibilities, evaluate students, or interact with patients or clients, just to name a few possible arenas in which illuminated individualism might be practiced. This would mean ensuring that hiring committees and admissions committees in colleges, to the greatest extent possible, include a diverse representation of persons from different racial and ethnic communities. Too often, merit is overlooked in those with backgrounds different from that of the dominant group—whites. What's more, there is evidence to suggest that diverse deliberation pools contribute to fairness not only because they inject new perspectives into the process that otherwise might be absent (in this case, the perspectives of people of color), but also because the presence of racial diversity in a deliberative body prompts more equanimity from whites: They consider information more deeply, try harder to be fair and generally make better, more thoughtful decisions.[290]

Among the things we could train evaluators to consider within institutional settings, one might include the way that racial identity status can affect one's access to prior opportunity (and thus the facially apparent credentials that a person may have, but which may not tell a complete story). Those in a position to hire employees or admit students to a particular school, could be trained to look at merit in a relative sense, by evaluating effort and drive (factors individuals can control) rather than mere outcomes, scores and end-of-the-line accomplishments, which are too often skewed by prior opportunity or the lack thereof. By thinking of job or college admission competitions as an eight-lap relay race in which some runners have had a five-lap head start, evaluative teams can more responsibly make fair judgments. Operating from a position of colorblindness, all that would matter is where an applicant ended up: their test score, their years of experience or other outcome variables, much as with a race in which all that mattered was who crossed the finish line first. But operating from a position of illuminated individualism and color-consciousness, those in charge of evaluating applicants would consider where someone ended up relative to their starting point. After all, a runner who starts out five laps behind but manages to close that gap to two laps, or three, or even four, is clearly the faster runner. So too, a college applicant who starts out with fewer advantages and less access to advanced classes and the most experienced teachers, but still manages to show promise on standardized tests and grades, could be considered equally or better qualified than their more privileged counterparts.

Additionally, illuminated individualism and color-consciousness would encourage those in evaluative positions to look for the kinds of intangible variables like perseverance and the ability to overcome setback, which are often not encompassed in traditional evaluation standards for jobs or school admissions, but which research has found are critical to future success. The importance of these abilities has been proven especially meaningful in academic settings, where students of color who score relatively low or mediocre on certain "cognitive" variables but high on "non-cognitive" indicia, like perseverance, end up doing just as well as (or better than) those with high cognitive scores.[291]

We can also make having experience in multicultural, diverse settings part of the qualification criteria used to select employees or students. In a nation that is becoming less white every day, having experience in diverse settings, working with people from a multitude of cultural, racial and ethnic backgrounds is no longer a luxury: It is increasingly becoming a necessity. Employers should place a premium on such experience, as should educational institutions. This would, by definition, boost the representation of persons of color in these institutions (since they are far more likely than whites to live in diverse communities and to have interacted with others across racial lines), but it would also help find and bring into various institutions a different kind of white person. Those whites who value cross-racial interaction and collaboration, have engaged in it and have demonstrated skill at working in these kind of settings would be in demand, while those who don't much care for such experiences, have tried to avoid them and/or haven't been successful in them, would be seen, viewed and treated as the anachronisms they are in the twenty-first century. By making multicultural experience a bona fide qualification requirement, institutions would also be able to insulate themselves from the threat of right-wing lawsuits over "preferential treatment" or "reverse discrimination." Yes, such a merit criterion would boost opportunity for people of color, and yes, it may possibly do so at the expense of some whites. But it would do so under a legitimate conception of qualifications, especially in an increasingly diverse and multicultural nation.

For colleges and universities, incorporating some kind of multicultural valuation and experience into the admissions process would be even easier. After all, most every college and university mission statement now includes reference to the value placed by the school on diversity, multicultural learning and the facilitation of global citizenship. Some even go further by pointing out their commitment to social justice and equity. With such missions in mind, schools would be well within their rights—and even ethical responsibilities—to evaluate applicants (students and potential faculty) not only on traditional criteria of academic and professional excellence but on their commitment to the school's mission as well. If the reason a college exists is to promote a certain set of values within and throughout the institution, that school should feel under no obligation to admit or hire persons whose values run counter to that mission, or even those who are merely ambivalent about it. And those schools would also be entitled, as a way to operationalize their mission statements, to require all students and faculty to demonstrate their commitments to that mission by way of some research or service project in order to graduate or receive tenure. As with employers, schools could make adherence to certain principles that facilitate antiracist commitment and equity part of what it means to be qualified to be a part of their respective families.

School officials should also take a proactive stance to undo some of the structural inequities that often manifest on their watch. They should end so-called ability tracking as it is currently practiced in primary and secondary schools. Not only is tracking often carried out in ways that limit opportunities for students of color and working-class students of all colors, it is also unrelated to better performance by higher-tracked students, as mentioned previously. What's more, evidence clearly indicates that the end of curricular stratification works to narrow racial performance gaps. In one Long Island school district, for instance, de-tracking has led to massive gains in graduation rates among students of color. A decade ago, fewer than a third of black and Latino students at the district's South Side High School were receiving regular New York State Regent's diplomas, compared to 98 percent of whites and Asians. By 2006, after adopting a policy of deliberate heterogeneous grouping, the black and Latino numbers had skyrocketed to 92 percent, and by 2009, 95 percent of all minority students in the school were receiving Regent's diplomas: far higher than the rate for white students statewide, and equal to the white rate at South Side.[292] Mixed-ability groupings in classrooms facilitate cooperative learning and allow teachers to develop skills at eliciting different learning styles and talents. Except in the case of students with profound and medically diagnosable learning disabilities, students should not be tracked separately. Furthermore, schools should carry out audits of their disciplinary practices to determine the degree of racial disparity in punishments, especially in racially integrated schools where they manifest most dramatically.

Additionally, teachers should be trained in methods for addressing racial achievement gaps, and especially on the research pertaining to the aforementioned subject of stereotype threat (also known as stereotype vulnerability). Claude Steele, formerly the head of the psychology department at Stanford, and his colleagues have long documented the way that members of stigmatized groups often underperform relative to their ability because of a fear that their performance (if subpar) might confirm a negative stereotype. So, for instance, black students, concerned about negative stereotypes regarding African American intelligence and academic ability—and especially when they are highly invested in doing well academically—will often experience additional stress as they take an important exam, and their performance will suffer as a result.[293]

While awareness of negative stereotypes about one's group can create anxiety that drives down test performance in academic settings, there are mechanisms that have been shown to diminish this vulnerability and close racial achievement gaps. Most of them are fairly simple, straightforward and importantly, cost-free. All they require is awareness on the part of educators and a willingness to be color-conscious so as to practice them. Among the ways teachers can reduce stereotype threat are the following:

- *Combine constructive criticism of the work done by students of color with regular and consistent reiteration of the teacher's belief in their potential.* Students of color report needing positive feedback, and especially a sense that their teachers believe in their ability, in order to put forth maximum effort in class. The fear that teachers don't view them as capable—no doubt part of being exposed to the fact that so many people hold negative stereotypes about their group—makes having a counterweight critical. Although praise should never be false (in other words, it helps no student to praise their effort if they put forth very little of it), transmitting positive messages about a student's abilities is one way to reduce stereotype threat and boost the academic performance of black and brown students.

- *Encourage group work, team projects, group studying and a collaborative approach to learning, rather than individual work and a competitive approach.* Research has indicated, and common sense dictates as well, that if students are experiencing stereotype threat, working with others on schoolwork and in study groups will facilitate higher achievement by de-stressing the academic setting. If a student knows that the weight of their success does not rest entirely on their own shoulders, because they are collaborating with others for a common goal, they can remain focused without feeling the pressure to "represent" for their racial or ethnic group.

- *Challenge students with high standards, rather than demean them with remediation.* Expectation levels are a crucial component in student success, especially the success of students of color. But too often schools treat students of color as damaged goods, not offering them high-level classes or challenging them to reach beyond their current level of achievement. Research by several scholars, especially Philip Uri Treisman, a mathematician at of the University of Texas, has found that challenging coursework, combined with the teamwork approach mentioned above, can result in large academic gains by black and Latino students and a significant reduction in academic achievement gaps between such students and whites.[294]

- *In keeping with this maxim, all middle schools should strive to enroll black students in eighth-grade algebra.* Too often these classes are not available at that age in schools with large numbers of black students, and at more integrated schools black students are not targeted for enrollment in algebra. But new research has found that the key to which math classes will be taken by black students in high school—and how well black students will do in those classes—is whether or not they took algebra in the last year of middle school. Exposure to algebra has even more impact for black students, in terms of future achievement, than prior math achievement itself.[295]

- *Teachers should reject the notion of "aptitude" and stress the malleability of intelligence and ability.* Too often, teachers and students alike buy into the notion that certain people just don't have the aptitude for certain subjects. In a society with deep-seated racial stereotypes, such thinking can easily take on a racial cast, leading teachers and students to believe that certain groups simply lack aptitude in particular areas. Yet research indicates that except for a very small band of profoundly learning-disabled persons, aptitude is largely mythical.[296] If teachers put students on notice from the beginning that everyone in a classroom can learn, that everyone is expected to and that intelligence and ability are "stretchable," they can do much to diminish stereotype vulnerability.[297]

- *Provide "centering" exercises in class that allow students of color to reflect favorably on their identities and values.* Some of the most exciting research on undoing stereotype vulnerability and closing racial achievement gaps was recently published in the journal *Science* by scholars at the University of Colorado at Boulder and Yale. The researchers describe having students engage in writing exercises, over the course of an academic semester, in which they were asked to write about some personally held value or values and explain why those were important to them. They were asked to do this several times throughout the semester, with the first writing exercise coming at the beginning of the academic year. Although this value-centering exercise had no measurable impact on the academic performance of white students, it boosted black achievement by one-quarter of a letter grade, and among those students who had been performing at the bottom of the class distribution (and thus were over-contributing to a racial performance gap relative to whites), grades rose by an entire half of a letter grade. This exercise, done only in the one semester, showed an ability to boost black grades, independent of other factors, for an entire two years.[298] Similar research has found that such exercises can, in and of themselves, reduce racial performance gaps by 40 percent.[299] By encouraging students to reflect on their identities (of which values are an important part) and view those identities as sources of strength and resolve, rather than as sources of negative stereotypes and stigmas, educators can get the best from students who may otherwise underperform.

- *Get students to see academic success as part of a larger project to undo institutionalized inequity and white supremacy*. All teaching is about more than the dispensing of knowledge alone. It performs a social function. The question is whether we understand that function, and how we define it. If we encourage success among students simply so they can eventually get a decent job, there is little reason to think they will be particularly inspired, especially if they see the job market as a stultifying, low-wage, dead-end avenue for them. On the other hand, if we make clear to students that inequity is a serious problem, and that it grows more entrenched every day that racial achievement gaps remain in place, students of color can experience their own success in connection with the larger, historic, liberatory struggle of their entire community. And there is evidence that this works. A math teacher in Cherry Creek, Colorado, for instance, recently helped prompt a substantial improvement in grades on the part of his black students by telling them in no uncertain terms that the system was an unjust racist one, and that there were people prepared to make them statistics. They could either collaborate with their own destruction or "blow up the statistics" and prove everyone wrong. His honesty, coupled with his belief in the students, prompted their grades to soar and inspired the creation of a mentoring group, set up by the black students themselves, to encourage one another to strive for excellence and to see their academic success in explicitly social and even revolutionary terms.[300] Elsewhere, education scholar Theresa Perry has noted how important it is for black students to see their individual accomplishment as linked to a larger collective narrative. But in order to make this work, schools must be race- and color-conscious and must understand the specific social determinants of African American achievement.[301]

Color-Consciousness and Public Policy

While there is much that can be done by individuals in their families, workplaces and schools to promote progressive color-consciousness, those private efforts could also use some support from public policy. Although private initiatives should never wait for public policy or governmental support before moving forward, raising the issue of making public policy more progressively color-conscious can and should go hand in hand with our private and personal commitments.

Among the potential public policies that those concerned about racial inequity should be pushing for in the short-term, one might include:

- *Racial Impact Statements.* Currently, when land is to be developed or certain types of public projects (even private ones) are undertaken, such as construction initiatives, an environmental impact statement typically has to be submitted demonstrating the effects of the proposed initiative on everything from pollution to groundwater contamination to the destruction of animal habitats. Yet when it comes to policies governing education, housing, taxes, economic stimulus legislation, bank bailouts, criminal justice or any other arena, there is no requirement that lawmakers be apprised of the potentially racially disparate impact of such legislation. By requiring lawmakers to think about such things and to document the possible outcomes of such-and-such effort on different racial communities, we could begin to build progressive color-consciousness into the process of lawmaking. Armed with the necessary information, lawmakers would then be able to determine if the benefits of a particular policy were compelling enough (in legal terms) to justify the racial disparities that might result, or if they should go back to the proverbial drawing board to fashion policies that would be more even-handed.

- *Mandatory availability analysis for all government-funded projects and the money to pay for it.* When government funds a project, from infrastructure repair to wetlands restoration to clean energy development, it typically initiates a bidding process for the work that needs to be contracted. Although the courts have limited the extent to which the state can directly steer contracts to persons of color and their companies, there is no reason that the government cannot at least ensure that before contracts are given out in a particular locale, an availability analysis has been performed that might tell us the number of contractors in the locale who are of color and available to work on whatever project is being funded. That way, if there is a significant disparity between the availability of such contractors, and their actual utilization on said projects, the state can re-bid the contracts or compel white primary contractors to subcontract with minority-owned businesses, as a direct result of evidence indicating their exclusion.

- *Bar companies found guilty of intentional racial discrimination from receiving government contracts, tax breaks or direct subsidies for a period of at least ten years.* Companies that are found to have discriminated are technically able to be barred from receiving government contracts. But rarely does this happen, and when it does, reinstatement is often quick, without much in the way of preconditions or policy changes at the company that might create a new, more equitable reality. Companies that are found guilty of intentional discrimination should be barred for at least a decade from receiving any public funds for contracts (or other subsidies) and required to show a detailed plan for how they intend to avoid such problems in the future, before they are allowed to once again benefit from public largesse and tax dollars.

- *Impose a two-strikes rule for the receipt of government contracts, tax breaks or subsidies for companies that are found guilty of discriminating, even unintentionally, by virtue of their policies, practices or procedures.* The law allows for racial discrimination to be proved even when intent is not demonstrated, if policies, practices and procedures within an institution have a disparate impact on persons of color. For such a practice to happen once might be possible as a matter of coincidence. But if a company's policies have a legally cognizable disparate impact on two separate occasions, it is much more likely that said policies were conceived for that purpose, even if intent cannot be conclusively shown. In such a situation, companies should be barred from ever again receiving federal government contracts, tax breaks or subsidies.

- In recognition of the newest research on the subject, *declare racism and racial discrimination to be public health issues facing people of color.* Often it is only when the government openly proclaims something to be a public health issue (smoking, obesity, AIDS, etc.) that lawmakers begin to take seriously their responsibilities to support efforts to address that problem. By declaring discrimination to be a public health issue, the state will be more likely to steer monies directly into research on methods for reducing racial health gaps, promoting cross-cultural competence in medical school trainings, undoing implicit bias among medical school students, and other initiatives. Such a declaration would also allow the government and even private institutions to better defend themselves against right-wing lawsuits. After all, when conservatives sue institutions for so-called "reverse discrimination," they argue that there is no compelling interest in targeting opportunity, for instance, to otherwise underserved people of color or in rectifying the effects of past and present discrimination. But if racism and discrimination—and the inequities they promote—are declared public health emergencies, it will be harder to argue that there is no compelling interest for such actions.

- And finally, *authorize a substantial amount of money, as part of the No Child Left Behind educational reform package, to train teachers nationwide on the various ways that racism and discrimination—both explicit and implicit—can indeed leave children behind, despite the best of teacher intentions.* Although No Child Left Behind is problematic in any number of ways, one of its biggest weaknesses is having a mandate for the closing of racial achievement gaps without the resources necessary to actually close them. Those resources, however, are not just material supplies—as is often believed—but also the resources of teacher preparation and an understanding of the specific dynamics that are contributing to the racial achievement gap in the first place. Unless teachers are trained, and consistently so, to recognize the social determiners of the achievement gap, even their best efforts at instruction may not help close those gaps. If the federal government is going to place mandates on local schools and school districts, it should see to it that teachers receive the kinds of preparation needed to make their efforts successful. These trainings should be developed in conjunction with educators in the nation's teaching colleges, utilizing the best practices known to them for preparing teachers to reduce racial achievement gaps.

In the long run, more thoroughgoing efforts will no doubt be necessary to rectify the substantial racial gaps in wealth, assets and overall well-being in America. Though the political will for such efforts hardly exists at present—and for that matter, an insufficient amount of public support would be likely at this stage—as we move forward, these are the kinds of things for which we should be building support.

- *Targeted stimulus and investment in communities where the residents are at least 50 percent persons of color, and all communities with poverty rates that are 150 percent of the national average.* It is one thing to pass economic stimulus legislation that aims to get a stalled economy moving forward again. It is quite another to do so with deliberativeness, in an attempt to target opportunity to the most underserved and impacted communities. Indeed, colorblind stimulus often marginalizes persons of color further, by steering government money to larger companies with inside connections on bidding and to construction companies with bad records on racial inclusion. Future stimulus efforts should be targeted to communities where the population is disproportionately of color and communities with poverty rates that are at least 50 percent above the national average. These are the very communities that are most likely to have been left behind in previous efforts—whether prior stimulus bills or older efforts like FHA and VA loans, or GI Bill benefits in the 1950s. By steering the money to development projects in these communities, the government can raise the economic profile of residents in these spaces. Although it is a race-conscious effort (in that the plan would target monies to communities of color), by also including any community (including white ones) with high poverty rates, the effort could avoid some of the political and legal ramifications of limiting the effort to black and brown spaces alone. Given the depression-level situations that exist in many of these communities, new stimulus legislation should be passed focusing on those spaces and aimed at creating jobs, growth and sustainable development in these locations. Priority should be given to green jobs projects both for purposes of environmental protection and for future energy independence.

- *Revise the Community Reinvestment Act (CRA) to cover all financial institutions, including independent mortgage brokers, and evaluate lending disparities not only in terms of census tracts and income but also in terms of race. Provide funding for credit counseling in any community with a high percentage of subprime loans, so that consumers will understand their obligations and rights as borrowers.* Currently the CRA only applies to federally insured banks and thrifts (savings and loans, etc.). As a result, independent mortgage brokers—who wrote a disproportionate share of the high-risk, subprime loans over the past decade—were able to engage in predatory lending in a way that regular banks could only have dreamed of. The brokers, knowing that they were going to sell the loans rather than keep them on their own books, had little incentive to worry about whether the borrowers could really afford the loans or what would happen down the line when the interest rates ballooned. By applying the CRA to all financial institutions, including these brokers, lenders would be more diligent about the way they wrote loans. And by providing federally funded credit counseling to borrowers, the government could reduce the risk that borrowers would get in over their heads, misunderstand the terms of the loans they were seeking and/or receiving, and ultimately find themselves in default. By analyzing lending patterns not only for disparate treatment of certain low-income communities (the current CRA standard) but also for disparate racial treatment generally (and then sanctioning lenders with records indicating discriminatory patterns of behavior), lenders would be more diligent about the way they treated borrowers of color, and less likely to discriminate. To not include race in the CRA evaluation standards would allow lenders to continue to gouge borrowers of color in non-poor communities, relative to their white counterparts, and borrowers of color who are not themselves poor. Because middle-class and higher-income borrowers of color are still far more likely than similar whites (and even lower-income whites) to be steered towards risky loans, protections of this nature are needed.

What all of these proposals have in common—and they are hardly an exhaustive list—is their rejection of colorblindness, as either a private practice or public policy agenda. They are rooted in a recognition that race matters, even in the so-called Age of Obama; that racial injustice continues to be a major national problem, despite the efforts of some, including the president and other post-racial liberals, to minimize the recognition of that truth. The rhetoric of racial transcendence upon which post-racial liberalism has relied for so long is a lie, and a dangerous one at that. It asks us to turn away from what the available evidence tells us, and instead to place our hopes upon good intentions, patriotic unity (however contrived) and a colorblind, universal public policy agenda that *by definition* cannot address and abolish racial inequity, no matter how fervently its supporters claim otherwise.

Only by facing reality and resolving to do better might we have any hope of undoing racism and its ill effects. Only by committing ourselves to color-consciousness—meaning an awareness of the *consequences* of color in a historically white-dominated nation—can we even theoretically begin to alter those consequences. Only by renouncing the see-no-evil mentality of colorblindness might we eventually come to a day when color will have no specific consequences, because racism will finally have been dismantled. Needless to say, that day is a long way off. So too, there is no guarantee that the proposals contained herein—whether the private and personal actions advocated first or the public policies that follow them—will bring about that day. But one thing we certainly know is this: In the absence of constructive action intended to truly equalize opportunities and life chances between whites and persons of color, institutionalized white privilege and supremacy will remain a fixed and normative condition. We will need bold thinking, and it is my hope that some of the recommendations contained in this book will spark others to take action and make proposals of their own.

I write these words on the first day of February 2010: exactly fifty years to the day since four young men—David Richmond, Joseph McNeil, Franklin McCain, and Ezell Blair Jr. (now known as Jibreel Khazan)—protested segregation by bravely occupying lunch counter seats in a Greensboro, North Carolina, Woolworth's store. As the college students planned their course of action, and even as they began their silent civil disobedience, they could have had no idea that within weeks, sit-ins would spread throughout the South, helping to push forward the civil rights struggle and ultimately facilitate the passage of anti-discrimination laws within just a few years. From their solitary action and those that followed—all of them private, voluntary and with no support whatsoever from the state (indeed, often in the face of intense government opposition to their actions)—these brave individuals changed the course of American history. They changed it just as surely as any president, any congressional representative, any senator or any titan of industry. They saw the problem clearly, they refused to be silenced by those who stood in the way of justice, and they acted.

Far be it from me to compare any of the recommendations I put forward in this book to the courageous acts of the Greensboro four, or the freedom riders, or the many hundreds, even thousands of souls who, in one form or another, took part in the early and most dangerous days of the freedom struggle. These prescriptions are not nearly as bold, in part because times have changed and now make necessary new strategies. They are not as confrontational perhaps, in part because the adversary today is also less blatant in its methods, and thus we need the precision of a scalpel where before a sledgehammer was the proper tool for forcing open opportunities and shattering the edifice of apartheid.

But as with the frontal assaults on institutional white supremacy that made possible the progress we have seen in the United States in the last fifty years, the suggestions I offer here take as a given one overriding truth: that, as Sweet Honey in the Rock sings, "We who believe in freedom cannot rest." Both the militancy of the early movement and the deliberate, if less radical steps advocated in these pages, proceed from the notion that standing still is never an option so long as inequities remain embedded in the very fabric of the culture. And both emanate from the realization that we cannot merely wait for the state or political leaders to act. We must take action ourselves. We must act on the recognition of that which we know to be true. We must move ahead and demand justice in our communities and institutions where we operate, with or without the blessing of the president or any other lawmakers. Even if post-racial liberalism continues to hold sway over the nation's politics for the foreseeable future, it need not continue to exercise its grip on *us*. If leaders will not lead, then the people must. Indeed, it has always been so, however much we may have forgotten it, or even if, sadly, we never learned this truth in our history classes.

Several years ago, when members of the St. Paul Community Baptist Church in Brooklyn began to perform the annual psychodrama known as *The MAAFA Suite* (MAAFA being a Kiswahili word for "catastrophe" and used by Dr. Marimba Ani to describe the Holocaust that beset African peoples beginning with the middle passage to the Americas), they offered a simple yet incredibly insightful motto for their work, and for what they hoped the performance would provide to black peoples seeing it: healing and the strengthening of their resolve. The motto was: "The way out is back through." In other words, there was no running from truth, no finessing it, no working around it as though it were not there. The injury has been real. It is still real today. We are still in the middle of the catastrophe, and in order to emerge on the other end, we will have to confront the beast without apology and without hesitation. There is no other way.

And we do this not out of guilt—after all, none of us created the system as we have found it—but out of responsibility: a responsibility to ourselves, to those who have gone before and to those who are coming after; out of responsibility to the nation and the planet, which in our better moments we claim to cherish. Guilt is what you feel for what you've *done*. Responsibility is what you take, because of who and what you *are*. Let us now commit to finding out who we are, and quickly, before it is too late.

ENDNOTES

1. The name of the report was officially "The Negro Family: The Case for National Action." It can be accessed online at www.dol.gov/oasam/programs/history/webid-meynihan.htm.
2. Stephen Steinberg, *Turning Back: The Retreat from Racial Justice in American Thought and Policy* (Boston: Beacon Press, 1995), p. 117.
3. Kenneth J. Neubeck and Noel A. Cazeneve, *Welfare Racism: Playing the Race Card Against America's Poor* (New York: Routledge, 2001).
4. Martin Gilens, *Why Americans Hate Welfare* (Chicago: University of Chicago Press, 1995).
5. William Julius Wilson, *The Declining Significance of Race* (Chicago: University of Chicago Press, 1978).
6. Steinberg (1995), p. 124.
7. William Julius Wilson, *The Truly Disadvantaged* (Chicago: University of Chicago Press, 1987).
8. Steinberg (1995), pp. 144–151.
9. Sleeper penned *Liberal Racism* in 1997 as a defense of colorblindness and the elevation of a shared American identity over race-based political organizing. Kahlenberg's principal contribution to the scholarship of post-racial liberalism was his 1996 book *The Remedy: Class, Race, and Affirmative Action*, in which he called for a reworking of affirmative action programs from race-based to class-based efforts. Richard Thompson Ford's 2008 book *The Race Card: How Bluffing About Bias Makes Race Relations Worse* seeks to separate what the author—a law professor at Stanford—considers legitimate cases of racism from those he deems invalid. Generally, he appears to believe the latter is a much larger category than the former. Elsewhere, he has called explicitly for a shift from race-based policies to address inequity to class-based efforts such as a New Deal–like Works Progress Administration, as with his May 17, 2009, editorial in the *Boston Globe* titled "The end of civil rights" www.boston.com/bostonglobe/ideas/articles/2009/05/17/the_end_of_civil_rights?mode=PF.
10. William Julius Wilson, *More Than Just Race: Being Black and Poor in the Inner City* (New York: W.W. Norton, 2009), Kindle Edition, locations 122–27.
11. Wilson (2009), Kindle Edition, locations 142–47.
12. Wilson (2009), Kindle Edition, locations 234–39.
13. George Lipsitz, *The Possessive Investment in Whiteness: How Whites Profit from Identity Politics* (Philadelphia: Temple University Press, 1998), pp. 6–7.
14. Barack Obama, *The Audacity of Hope: Thoughts on Reclaiming the American Dream* (New York: Three Rivers Press, 2006), pp. 10–11.
15. Obama (2006), pp. 96–98.
16. Obama (2006), p. 177.
17. Obama, for instance, discussed his grandfather's ability to procure an FHA home loan and take advantage of the GI Bill during his 2004 speech to the Democratic

National Convention. www.washingtonpost.com/wp-dyn/articles/A19751-2004Jul27.html.

18. See, for instance, Ira Katznelson, *When Affirmative Action Was White: An Untold History of Racial Inequality in Twentieth-Century America* (New York: W.W. Norton and Company, 2005), 22; Philip F. Rubio, *A History of Affirmative Action: 1619–2000* (Jackson, MS: University Press of Mississippi, 2000).
19. Mark R. Warren, *Crossing Over the Color Line: How White Activists Embrace Racial Justice* (New York: Oxford University Press, forthcoming, 2010).
20. Obama (2006): p. 177.
21. Obama (2006), p. 245.
22. Michael K. Brown, Martin Carnoy, Elliott Currie, Troy Duster, David B. Oppenheimer, Marjorie M. Shultz and David Wellman, *Whitewashing Race: The Myth of a Color-Blind Society* (Berkeley, CA: University of California Press, 2003), p. 74.
23. Obama (2006), pp. 246–7.
24. Paul Street, *Barack Obama and the Future of American Politics* (Boulder, CO: Paradigm Publishers, 2008), p. 49.
25. Interestingly, if you type the words "The Speech" into Google, the first two references are to Obama's "More Perfect Union" race speech. In YouTube, a clip of the same speech is the first clip to pop up when the same words are entered. Just last year, a collection of essays was published on the subject, titled *The Speech: Race and Barack Obama's "A More Perfect Union"* edited by Vanderbilt professor T. Denean Sharpley-Whiting (New York: Bloomsbury, 2009).
26. For a full text of "A More Perfect Union," go to: www.huffingtonpost.com/2008/03/18/obama-race-speech-read-t_n_92077.html.
27. Fox News Poll/Opinions Dynamics, April 30, 2008. www.foxnews.com/projects/pdf/043008_release_web.pdf.
28. CBS News Poll/*The New York Times*, "Race Relations and Politics," April 3, 2008. www.cbsnews.com/htdocs/pdf/Mar08c-Race.pdf.
29. Douglas S. Massey and Nancy A. Denton, *American Apartheid: Segregation and the Making of the Underclass* (Cambridge, MA: Harvard University Press, 1993).
30. Adam Mansbach, "The Audacity of Post-Racism," in *The Speech*, ed. Sharpley-Whiting, p. 69.
31. Sylvia Hurtado and Christine Navia, "Reconciling College Access and the Affirmative Action Debate," in *Affirmative Action's Testament of Hope*, ed. Mildred Garcia (Albany, NY: SUNY Press, 1997), p. 115.
32. For a full discussion of affirmative action and a point-by-point refutation of conservative attacks on the concept, please see my earlier book *Affirmative Action: Racial Preference in Black and White* (New York: Routledge, 2005).
33. Mansbach (2009), p. 75.
34. Connie Schultz, "His Grandmother, My Father, Your Uncle . . ." in *The Speech*, ed. Sharpley-Whiting, pp. 104–5.
35. Jonathan Kaufman, "Whites Great Hope? Barack Obama and the Dream of a Color-Blind America," *Wall Street Journal*, November 10, 2007, A1.

36. One could also make the argument that Obama's post-racial approach bore very little fruit, even for him personally. Yes, he managed to gain the votes of a few percentage points' more whites than any Democrat in forty years, but there is no way to know if this was due to his avoidance of race matters so much as the uniquely bad economy against which he was running, and the uptick in the youth vote, which went so dramatically in his favor. Indeed, overall, white voter turnout was down. Nationally, whites cast 700,000 fewer votes in 2008 than they had four years earlier. It was really a dramatic increase in the black and Latino vote that may have made the difference in the end for Obama. Indeed, there were 3 million more black votes in 2008 than in 2004. See Mike Davis, "Obama at Manassas," *New Left Review*, March–April 2009, p. 24.
37. "Transcript: President Obama's 100th-Day Press Briefing," *New York Times*, April 29, 2009. www.nytimes.com/2009/04/29/us/politics/29text-obama.html?pagewanted=1&_r=1.
38. Darlene Superville, "Obama Defends Himself Against Black Critics," *The Huffington Post* (December 21, 2009). www.huffingtonpost.com/2009/12/21/obama-defends-himself-aga_n_399819.html.
39. George Picard, "Racial Spoils in Obama's America," *American Thinker* (January 6, 2010), www.americanthinker.com/2010/01/racial_spoils_in_obamas_americ.html; Paul Sperry, "Obama's Stealth Reparations," *FrontPageMag.com* (October 28, 2008). It is interesting to note that among the "reparations" examples offered up by Picard in the cited column is the supposed desire on the part of the Obama administration to scrap work requirements in the 1996 welfare reform bill, passed under President Clinton. Because African Americans are disproportionately likely to receive public assistance (because they are disproportionately poor), loosening work requirements for those receiving aid would, according to Picard, be tantamount to a disparate benefit for blacks and thus untoward, perhaps even unconstitutional. But of course, by this logic, which Picard naturally fails to follow to its ultimate conclusion, the *passage* of the welfare reform bill, and the imposition of work requirements, would *also* be properly seen as disparate in impact, this time *against* blacks, and would have been invalid as well. Likewise, conservative calls for estate tax cuts or capital gains tax cuts would be illegitimate racial handouts to whites, since whites are far more likely to pay these taxes, being disproportionately among the wealthiest individuals, therefore subject to paying them. It is doubtful that conservatives like Picard would much appreciate where their own argumentation leads.
40. Media Matters for America, "Glenn Beck: Obama agenda driven by 'reparations' and desire to 'settle old racial scores,'" July 23, 2009. http://mediamatters.org/mmtv/200907230040.
41. This statement, which Bond has made on several occasions, is found in a 2003 speech, excerpts of which are available on the Internet at www.turningpointtechnologies.com/clients/services/pdf.php?id=41.
42. The Gallup Organization, Gallup Poll Social Audit, *Black-White Relations in the United States, 2001 Update* (July 10, 2001), p. 7–9.

43. Leonard Steinhorn and Barbara Diggs-Brown, *By the Color of Our Skin: The Illusion of Integration and the Reality of Race* (New York: Dutton, 1999), p. 110.
44. Warren (forthcoming, 2010).
45. Brown et al. (2003), p. 35.
46. Michael Luo, "In Job Hunt, College Degree Can't Close Racial Gap," *The New York Times* (November 30, 2009), www.nytimes.com/2009/12/01/us/01race.html?_r=1
47. United States Department of Labor, Bureau of Labor Statistics, *Employment and Earnings, September 2009.* 56:9, 25. The racial gaps in this Table (number A-17) appear a bit smaller than what is being claimed here. This is because Hispanics are not broken out separately from the white totals, and about 94 percent of all Hispanics are classified in labor department data and census data as "white" when racial categories are being identified. To extract Latinos from the white totals for a more accurate picture of the white–person of color unemployment ratios, I simply multiplied the number of Latinos who have college degrees and are unemployed, provided in the table, by 0.94. Then I subtracted that number (about 193,000) from the white totals for persons with degrees who were unemployed, since that number would represent Latinos. I did the same calculation for the civilian labor force numbers: multiplying the Latino number by 0.94 and subtracting that amount from the white civilian labor force numbers to arrive at non-Hispanic white numbers for each. From there, I divided the unemployment number for non-Hispanic whites by the non-Hispanic white civilian labor force number, to determine the unemployment rate for non-Hispanic whites. When Latinos are subtracted from the white numbers, the white unemployment rate drops from 4.8 percent to 4.6.
48. "Racial disparities persist in higher-paying jobs," Associated Press (April 27, 2009), www.msnbc.msn.com/id/30437468/print/1/displaymode/1098.
49. Carmen DeNavas-Walt, Bernadette D. Proctor and Jessica C. Smith, U.S. Census Bureau, Current Population Reports, P60-235, *Income, Poverty, and Health Insurance Coverage in the United States: 2007* (U.S. Government Printing Office, Washington, DC, 2008).
50. United States Department of Labor, Bureau of Labor Statistics, *Employment and Earnings, September 2009.* 56:9, p. 46.
51. United States Department of Labor (2009), p. 209.
52. Associated Press, "Racial disparity persists in higher paying jobs," *MSNBC.com* (April 27, 2009), www.msnbc.com/id/30437468.
53. "Major Study of Asian Americans Debunks 'Model Minority' Myth," *ScienceDaily* (November 12, 2008), www.sciencedaily.com/releases/2008/11/081112101339.htm.
54. Richard Morin, "Misperceptions Cloud Whites' View of Blacks," *Washington Post* (July 11, 2001), A1.
55. Kaiser Family Foundation, *Survey of Race, Ethnicity and Medical Care: Public Perceptions and Experiences* (Washington, DC: Henry J. Kaiser Family Foundation), October 1999.
56. United States Department of Commerce, Bureau of the Census, *Statistical Abstracts of the United States, 2002* (Washington, DC, 2002), Table 137: p. 102.

57. Shawna Orzechowski and Peter Sepielli, *Net Worth and Asset Ownership of Households: 1998 and 2000*. Current Population Reports, P70-88 (United States Census Bureau, Washington, DC, May, 2003), pp. 2, 13–15. Those who dismiss data on wealth gaps between whites and blacks sometimes claim that these gaps—because they represent households—simply reflect the fact that black households are more likely to contain only one adult. As such, they will naturally have less wealth when compared to a white family with two adults in the home. But this claim has little merit. Although single-parent household status certainly affects black *income* relative to white income (since only one income earner will make less, typically, than two), it has little impact on wealth. While one can make income by working, one can't simply "make" wealth and assets. Given that these are mostly transferred from prior generations, for a black woman and black man to marry, for instance, would result in no net boost in wealth (or at least very little), as neither would be likely to have inherited any intergenerational bequest. Zero plus zero is zero.
58. Melvin Oliver and Thomas Shapiro, *Black Wealth/White Wealth: A New Perspective on Racial Inequality* (New York: Routledge, 1996), p. 96.
59. Thomas Shapiro, *The Hidden Cost of Being African American: How Wealth Perpetuates Inequality* (New York: Oxford University Press, 2004), p. 55.
60. Orzechowski and Sepielli (2003), p. 14.
61. Shapiro (2004), p. 38.
62. David H. Swinton, "Racial Inequality and Reparations," in *The Wealth of Races: The Present Value of Benefits from Past Injustices*, ed., Richard F. America (New York: Greenwood Press, 1990), pp. 153–16.
63. For information on extra-judicial and terroristic white violence against communities of color, see Massey and Denton (1993) and James Clarke, *The Lineaments of Wrath: Race, Violent Crime and American Culture* (Edison, NJ: Transaction Publishers, 2001).
64. Brown et al. (2003), p. 30; Monica McDermott, *Working-Class White: The Making and Unmaking of Race Relations* (Berkeley, CA: University of California Press, 2006), p. 27.
65. Brown et al. (2003), pp. 76–77; Douglas S. Massey, *Categorically Unequal: The American Stratification System* (New York: Russell Sage Foundation, 2007), p. 63.
66. Karen Brodkin, *How Jews Became White Folks: And What That Says About Race in America* (Brunswick, NJ: Rutgers University Press, 1998), p. 44.
67. Brown et al. (2003), pp. 76–77.
68. Brown et al. (2003), p. 28.
69. Claude S. Fischer, Michael Hout, Martin Sanchez Jankowski, Samuel R. Lucas, Ann Swidler and Kimm Voss, *Inequality by Design: Cracking the Bell Curve Myth* (Princeton, NJ: Princeton University Press, 1996), p. 179.
70. Joe Feagin, "Toward an Integrated Theory of Systemic Racism," in *The Changing Terrain of Race and Ethnicity*, eds. Maria Krysan and Amanda E. Lewis (New York: Russell Sage Foundation, 2004), pp. 213–14.
71. Shapiro (2004), p. 190.

72. Brown et al. (2003), pp. 77–78.
73. Katznelson (2005), p. 113.
74. Brown et al. (2003), p. 79.
75. Shapiro (2004), pp. 61, 65.
76. Shapiro (2004), pp. 62, 64.
77. Shapiro (2004), pp. 71, 67.
78. Douglas S Massey, Camille Z. Charles, Garvey Lundy and Mary J. Fischer, *The Source of the River: The Social Origins of Freshmen at America's Selective Colleges and Universities* (Princeton, NJ: Princeton University Press, 2003), pp. 43, 156.
79. General Accounting Office, "Information on Minority Targeted Scholarships," B251634 (Washington, DC: U.S. Government Printing Office, January 1994).
80. Stephen L. Carter, "Color-Blind and Color-Active," *The Recorder* (January 3, 1992).
81. "Stat of the Week," *Journal of Blacks in Higher Education* (Weekly Bulletin), January 21, 2010.
82. Although some suggest that Obama's elevation to the Presidency (combined with his obvious erudition, intelligence and abilities, recognized even by many of his political adversaries) might cause whites to rethink their stereotypes about African Americans, the available evidence doesn't bode particularly well for this optimistic view. According to that research, when we are confronted by people whose personas tend to contradict the group-based assumptions we would normally have for them, we tend to make up stories in our own minds, allowing the apparent inconsistency to gel, rather than rethink the stereotype altogether. In other words, in the face of stereotypes, evidence that contradicts that stereotype tends to be compartmentalized in a part of the brain marked "exception to the rule." But the rule remains the same. See, Gary Blasi, "Advocacy Against the Stereotype: Lessons from Cognitive Social Psychology," in Gregory S. Parks, Shayne Jones and W. Jonathan Cardi, *Critical Race Realism: Intersections of Psychology, Race and Law* (New York: New Press, 2008). Thus President Obama, in and of himself, can do little to challenge white folks' thinking about blacks.
83. McDermott, *(*2007).
84. Houts Picca and Feagin (2007), pp. 7, 18, 101.
85. Lawrence D. Bobo, "Inequalities That Endure? Racial Ideology, American Politics and the Peculiar Role of the Social Sciences," in Maria Krysan and Amanda E. Lewis, *The Changing Terrain of Race and Ethnicity* (New York: Russell Sage Foundation, 2004), p. 20.
86. Judith R. Blau, *Race in the Schools: Perpetuating White Dominance?* (Boulder, CO: Lynne Rienner Press, 2003), p. 53.
87. Joe R. Feagin, *The White Racial Frame: Centuries of Racial Framing and Counter-Framing* (New York: Routledge, 2009), p. 92.
88. Massey (2007), p. 69.
89. Camille Charles, "The Dynamics of Racial Residential Segregation," *Annual Review of Sociology* 29 (2003), pp. 167–207.
90. Steinhorn and Diggs-Brown (1999), p. 101.

91. Steinhorn and Diggs-Brown (1999), p. 41.
92. Dennis Rome, *Black Demons: The Media's Depiction of the African American Male Criminal Stereotype* (New York: Praeger, 2004).
93. "Negative Perception of Blacks Rises With More News Watching, Studies Say," *ScienceDaily* (July 17, 2008), www.sciencedaily.com/releases/2008/07/080717134527.htm.
94. B.W. Burston, D. Jones and P. Robertson-Saunders, "Drug Use and African-Americans: Myth Versus Reality," *Journal of Alcohol and Drug Education.* 40(2) (1995), pp. 19–39.
95. Substance Abuse and Mental Health Services Administration (SAMHSA), *Summary of Findings from the 2000 National Household Survey on Drug Abuse* (Office of Applied Studies, Department of Health and Human Services, Rockville, MD., 2001), Table F.14; SAMHSA, *Results from the 2002 National Survey on Drug Use and Health.* Also *Summary of Findings from the National Household Survey on Drug Abuse* (Office of Applied Studies, Department of Health and Human Services, Rockville, MD, 2003); Centers for Disease Control and Prevention, *Youth Risk Behavior Surveillance—United States, 2005. Surveillance Summaries* (Washington, DC., June 9, 2006).
96. Americans for American Values, "What is Implicit Bias?: Bias by Any Other Name," http://americansforamericanvalues.org/unconsciousbias.
97. Though some have claimed that implicit bias tests are flawed—in that they can only predict behavior in a lab or other experimental setting and may bear no connection to real-world discriminatory behavior—additional examinations of more than 180 different studies on the instruments have found that IATs actually can predict behavior outside the testing situation, and far more accurately, for instance, than self-report surveys. "Test That Found Widespread Unconscious Racial Bias Validated," *ScienceDaily* (June 18, 2009), www.sciencedaily.com/releases/2009/06/090617142120.htm.
98. Joe R. Feagin, *Systemic Racism* (New York: Routledge, 2006), p. 26; William A. Cunningham, Marcia K. Johnson, Carol L. Raye, J. Chris Gatenby, John C. Gore and Mahzarin R. Banaji, "Separable Neural Components in the Processing of Black and White Faces," *Psychological Science* 15:12 (2004); Elizabeth A. Phelps, Kevin J. O'Connor, William A. Cunningham, E. Sumie Funayama, J. Christopher Gatenby, John C. Gore, and Mahzarin R. Banaji, "Performance on Indirect Measures of Race Evaluation Predicts Amygdala Activation," *Journal of Cognitive Neuroscience* 12:5 (2000).
99. Theodore Eisenberg and Sheri Lynn Johnson, "Implicit Racial Attitudes of Death Penalty Lawyers," *DePaul Law Review* 53 (2004), p. 1539.
100. Feagin (2009), p. 111.
101. Birt L. Duncan, "Differential Social Perception and Attributes of Intergroup Violence: Testing the Lower Limits of Stereotyping of Blacks," *Journal of Personality and Social Psychology* (1976).
102. H. Andrew Sager and Janet Wind Schofield, "Racial and Behavioral Cues in Black

and White Children's Perceptions of Ambiguously Aggressive Acts," *Journal of Personality and Social Psychology* (1980).

103. Feagin (2009), p. 94
104. Joshua Correll, Bernadette Park, Charles M. Judd and Bernd Wittenbrink, "The Police Officer's Dilemma: Using Ethnicity to Disambiguate Potentially Threatening Individuals," *Journal of Personality and Social Psychology* 83:6 (2002); Keith B. Payne, "Prejudice and Perception: The Role of Automatic and Controlled Processes in Misperceiving a Weapon," *Journal of Personality and Social Psychology* (2001); and Jennifer L. Eberhardt, Phillip Atiba Goff, Valerie J. Purdie and Paul G. Davies, "Seeing Black: Race, Crime and Visual Processing," *Journal of Personality and Social Psychology* 87:6 (December, 2004).
105. Justin D. Levinson, "Forgotten Racial Equality: Implicit Bias, Decision-Making and Misremembering," *Duke Law Journal* 57 (November, 2007).
106. Franklin D. Gilliam Jr. and Shanto Iyangar, "Prime Suspects: The Influence of Local Television News on the Viewing Public," *American Journal of Political Science* 44 (2000).
107. Steinhorn and Diggs-Brown (1999), p. 155.
108. M. Peffley, T. Shields and B. Williams, "The Intersection of Race and Crime in Television News Stories: An Experimental Study," *Political Communication* 13 (1996).
109. Linda Hamilton Krieger and Susan T. Fiske, "Behavioral Realism in Employment Discrimination Law: Implicit Bias and Disparate Treatment," *California Law Review* 94:997 (2006).
110. Richard Thompson Ford, "The End of Civil Rights," *The Boston Globe* (May 17, 2009), www.boston.com/bostonglobe/ideas/articles/2009/05/17/the_end_of_civil_rights?mode=PF.
111. ABC News/Washington Post Poll: Race Relations, "Fewer Call Racism a Major Problem Though Discrimination Remains," January 19, 2009.
112. This methodology is a fairly conservative one, as it presumes that the baseline utilization of people of color in a given industry and locale is not itself indicative of discrimination, and only presumes discrimination in cases wherein a company performs well below that baseline. In other words, it is possible that discrimination across an entire industry, and in a particular locale, is so common that people of color may be underrepresented among all firms in an area. Yet the Blumrosen study would not have counted such cases as evidence of discrimination, because they were operating from the assumption that the area/industry norm was itself a valid indicator of availability and utilization.
113. Alfred Blumrosen and Ruth Blumrosen, *The Reality of Intentional Job Discrimination in Metropolitan America: 1999* (New Jersey: Rutgers University, 1999), www.eeo1.com/1999_NR/Title.pdf.
114. Marianne Bertrand and Sendhil Mullainathan, "Are Emily and Greg More Employable Than Lakisha and Jamal? A Field Experiment in Labor Market Discrimination" (June 20, 2004), http://post.economics.harvard.edu/faculty/mullainathan/papers/emilygreg.pdf.

115. Devah Pager and Bruce Western, *Race at Work: Realities of Race and Criminal Record in the NYC Job Market*, paper presented at the New York City Commission on Human Rights conference, Schomburg Center for Research in Black Culture (December 9, 2005).
116. Devah Pager, *Marked: Race, Crime and Finding Work in an Era of Mass Incarceration* (Chicago: University of Chicago Press, 2007).
117. "New Data Exposes Dramatic Racial Discrimination in U.S. Advertising Industry," *Earth Times* (January 8, 2009). www.earthtimes.org/articles/show/new-data-exposes-dramatic-racial-discrimination-in-us-advertising-industry,673479.shtml.
118. Restaurant Opportunities Center of New York, *The Great Service Divide: Occupational Segregation and Inequality in the New York City Restaurant Industry* (March 31, 2009).
119. Applied Research Center, *Race and Recession: How Inequity Rigged the Economy and How to Change the Rules* (Oakland, CA: Applied Research Center, May 2009), p. 21.
120. LeAnn Lodder, Scott McFarland, Diana White, Paul Street and Dennis Kass, *Racial Preference and Suburban Employment Opportunities: A Report on "Matched-Pair" Tests of Chicago-Area Retailers* (Chicago: Legal Assistance Foundation of Metropolitan Chicago and the Chicago Urban League, 2003); Philip Moss and Chris Tilly, *Stories Employers Tell: Race, Skill and Hiring in America* (New York: Russell Sage Foundation, 2003).
121. Brown et al. (2003), p. 84–85.
122. Moss and Tilly (2003), 106.
123. Brown et al. (2003), 85.
124. Steve McDonald, Non Lin and Dan Ao, "Networks of Opportunity: Gender, Race and Job Leads," *Social Problems* 56:3 (August 2009), p. 385–402.
125. Fischer et al. (1996), p. 182.
126. Deirdre Royster, *Race and the Invisible Hand: How White Networks Exclude Black Men from Blue-Collar Jobs* (Berkeley, CA: University of California Press, 2003).
127. Barbara Bergmann, *In Defense of Affirmative Action* (New York: Basic Books, 1996), pp. 72–74, 79; Stephanie A. Goodwin, "Situational Power and Interpersonal Dominance Facilitate Bias and Inequality," *Journal of Social Issues* (Winter,1998); Moss and Tilly (2003).
128. Patrick L. Mason, "Identity matters: inter- and intra-racial disparity and labor market outcomes," (MPRA paper, University Library of Munich, May 8, 2009).
129. Eduardo Bonilla-Silva and Karen S. Glover, " 'We are All Americans': The Latin Americanization of Race Relations in the United States," in *The Changing Terrain of Race and Ethnicity*, eds. Maria Krysan and Amanda E. Lewis (New York: Russell Sage Foundation, 2004), pp. 158–161.
130. *A Snapshot of "A Portrait of Chinese Americans," Key Findings* (Washington, DC, and College Park, MD: Organization of Chinese Americans and the Asian American Studies Program, University of Maryland, November, 2008), p. 5.
131. Terrance Reeves and Claudette Bennett, "The Asian and Pacific Islander

Population in the United States: March 2002," P20-540, *Current Population Reports*, (Washington, DC:U.S. Census Bureau, May, 2003).

132. Rosalind S. Chou and Joe R. Feagin, *The Myth of the Model Minority: Asian Americans Facing Racism* (Boulder, CO: Paradigm Publishers, 2008), p. 12.
133. Nancy Rivera Brooks, "Study Attacks Belief in Asian American Affluence, Privilege," *San Jose Mercury News* (May 19, 1994), 1A.
134. Richard Thompson Ford, "A Primer on Racism," *Slate* (September 30, 2009), www.slate.com/toolbar.aspx?action=print&id=2231002.
135. "Housing Discrimination Complaints at an All-Time High," Press Release, Department of Housing and Urban Development (April 3, 2007), www.hud.gov/news/release.cfm?content=pr07-032.cfm.
136. Massey and Denton (1993), p. 200; Deborah L. McKoy and Jeffrey M. Vincent, "Housing and Education: The Inextricable Link," in *Segregation: The Rising Costs for America*, eds. James H. Carr and Nandinee K. Kutty (New York: Routledge, 2008), p. 128.
137. Applied Research Center (2009), pp. 37–39.
138. Kathleen C. Engel and Patricia A. McCoy, "The CRA Implications of Predatory Lending," *Fordham Urban Law Journal* 29:4 (2002), pp. 1571–1606.
139. Michael Powell and Janet Roberts, "Minorities Affected Most as NY Foreclosures Rise," *New York Times* (May 16, 2009).
140. "Special Report: Banking on Misery—Citigroup, Wall Street and the Fleecing of the South," *Facing South* 51 (June 5, 2003).
141. Michael Powell, "Bank Accused of Pushing Mortgage Deals on Blacks," *New York Times* (June 6, 2009), www.nytimes.com/2009/06/07/us/07baltimore.html?_r=1.
142. Peter Dreier and John Atlas, "The GOP Scapegoats ACORN," *CBS News*, October 25, 2008, www.cbsnews.com/stories/2008/10/24/opinion/main4544472.shtml.
143. Massey (2007), p. 76.
144. Fischer et al. (1996), p. 196.
145. Sam Spatter, "Fair Housing Partnership Study: Blacks Still face Mortgage Bias," *Pittsburgh Tribune Review* (November 25, 2009), www.pittsburghlive.com/x/pittsburghtrib/business/s_654803.html.
146. John Yinger, *Closed Doors: Opportunities Lost: The Continuing Costs of Housing Discrimination* (New York: Russell Sage Foundation, 1995), p. 138; Valerie Martinez-Ebers, "Latino Interests in Education, Health and Criminal Justice Policy," *Political Science and Politics* (September 2000).
147. Paul Street, *Segregated Schools: Educational Apartheid in Post-Civil Rights America* (New York: Routledge, 2005), pp. 13–15.
148. Amanda Paulson, "Resegregation of U.S. Schools Deepening," *Christian Science Monitor* (January 25, 2008), www.csmonitor.com/2008/0125/p01s01-ussc.html?page=1.
149. Martinez-Ebers (2000); Gary Orfield et al., "Deepening Segregation in American Public Schools: A Special Report from the Harvard Project on School Desegregation," *Equity & Excellence in Education* 30 (1997), pp. 5–24.

150. C Kirabo Jackson, "Student Demographics, Teacher Sorting and Teacher Quality: Evidence from the End of School Desegregation," *Journal of Labor Economics* 27:2 (2009), p. 213.
151. Blasi (2008), p. 45.
152. Linda Darling-Hammond, "Unequal Opportunity: Race and Education," *Brookings Review* (Spring, 1998), p. 31.
153. Stephen J. Ceci, "How Much Does Schooling Influence General Intelligence and Its Cognitive Components? A Reassessment of the Evidence," *Developmental Psychology* 27 (1991), pp. 703–722.
154. Jawanza Kunjufu, *Black Students, Middle Class Teachers* (Chicago: African American Images, 2002), p. 57.
155. Massey and Denton (1993), pp. 153, 86.
156. Massey and Denton (1993), p. 153.
157. Vickie L. Shavers and Brenda S. Shavers, "Racism and Health Inequity Among Americans," *Journal of the National Medical Association* 98:3 (March, 2006), p. 388.
158. The Civil Rights Project, "Racial Inequity in Special Education" (UCLA: The Civil Rights Project, June, 2002), www.civilrightsproject.ucla.edu/research/specialed.IDEA_paper02.php .
159. Shavers and Shavers (2006), p. 389.
160. The Civil Rights Project (2002).
161. Janese Free, "The Relationship Between School Tracking and Race From a Social Psychological Perspective," paper presented at the Annual Meeting of the American Sociological Association, Montreal (August 11, 2006), www.allacademic.com/meta/p105226_index.html; Rebecca Gordon, *Education and Race* (Oakland, CA: Applied Research Center, 1998), pp. 48–49; Claude S. Fischer et al. (1996), pp. 164–65; Steinhorn and Diggs-Brown (1999), p. 47.
162. Gary Orfield and Susan Eaton, *Dismantling Desegregation: The Quiet Reversal of Brown v Board of Education* (New York: The New Press, 1996), p. 68.
163. Asian Law Caucus, "Facts and Fantasies About UC Berkeley Admissions: A Critical Evaluation of Regent John Moores' Report" (Berkeley, CA: Asian Law Caucus, October 24, 2003).
164. Andrew Grant-Thomas, "Accusing Someone of Racism Squashes the Likelihood of Fruitful Dialogue Like a Bug," *Huffington Post* (January 7, 2010), www.huffingtonpost.com/andrew-grantthomas-phd/accusing-someone-of-racis_b_414743.html.
165. "Ability Grouping in Elementary School Hampers Minority Students' Literacy," *ScienceDaily* (April 21, 2009), www.sciencedaily.com/releases/2009/04/090421120904.htm.
166. Free (2006), p. 11.
167. Jeannie Oakes, *Keeping Track: How Schools Structure Inequality* (New Haven, CT: Yale University Press, 1985), pp. 8–11.
168. Oakes (1985), pp. 101.
169. Linda Darling-Hammond, "From 'Separate but Equal' to 'No Child Left Behind': The

Collision of New Standards and Old Inequalities," in *Many Children Left Behind*, eds. Deborah Meier and George Wood (Boston: Beacon Press, 2004), p. 9.

170. Street (2005), p. 78.
171. Darling-Hammond (2004), p. 4.
172. Street (2005), p. 81.
173. Sarah Goff, "When Education Ceases to Be Public: The Privatization of the New Orleans School System, Post–Hurricane Katrina," submitted in partial fulfillment of the requirements for the degree of Master's of Science in Urban Studies, University of New Orleans (May, 2009).
174. Darling-Hammond (2004), 10.
175. Russell J. Skiba et al., *The Color of Discipline: Sources of Racial and Gender Disproportionality in School Punishment* (Indiana Education Policy Center, Research Report SRS1, June 2000), pp. 6, 13.
176. U.S. Centers for Disease Control and Prevention, *Youth Risk Behavior Surveillance System: Youth 2003 Online, Comprehensive Results* (2004), http://apps.nccd.cdc.gov/yrbss.
177. Skiba et al. (2000), p. 4.
178. Russell Skiba, Robert S. Michael, Abra Carroll Nardo and Reece L. Peterson, "The Color of Discipline: Sources of Racial and Gender Disproportionality in School Punishment," *The Urban Review* 34:4 (December 2002), p. 333.
179. Mica Pollock, *Colormute: Race Talk Dilemmas in an American School* (Princeton, NJ: Princeton University Press, 2004).
180. Adam Serwer, "The De-Facto Segregation of Health Care," *American Prospect* (August 21, 2009), http://prospect.org/cs/articles?article=the_defacto_segregation_of_health_care; Ryan Blitstein, "Racism's Hidden Toll," *Miller-McCune* (June, 2009) http://miller-mccune.com/health/racisms-hidden-toll-1268?article_page=1.
181. Joseph L. Graves, *The Race Myth: Why We Pretend Race Exists in America* (New York: Dutton, 2004), p. 133.
182. "Racism as the Root Cause of Infant Mortality," *Racism Review* (July 6, 2008), www.racismreview.com/blog/2008/07/06/racism-as-the-root-cause-of-infant-mortality/. This data is provided by Barbara Ferrer, Executive Director of the Boston Public Heath Commission, in a fascinating PowerPoint presentation that can be viewed/downloaded at the above link.
183. Serwer (2009).
184. "Racism as the Root Cause of Infant Mortality" (2008).
185. "Racism as the Root Cause of Infant Mortality" (2008).
186. Ryan Blitstein, "Racism's Hidden Toll," Miller-McCune (June 2009), http://miller-mccune.com/health/racisms-hidden-toll-1268?article_page=1.
187. "Racism as the Root Cause of Infant Mortality" (2008). It should also be noted here that African Americans typically have lower rates of cigarette use than whites, lower rates of heavy alcohol use, and rates of narcotic use that are roughly equivalent to those of whites. Thus, when it comes to behaviors that often correlate with compromised health, blacks are no more likely and sometimes less likely to indulge in those behaviors than whites are.

188. "Unnatural Causes" (2008), p. 2.
189. "Study Suggests Racial Discrimination Harms Health," *ScienceDaily* (September 9, 2005), www.sciencedaily.com/releases/2005/09/050909074111.htm.
190. A. Geronimus, "Understanding and eliminating racial inequalities in women's health in the United States: The role of the weathering conceptual framework," *Journal of the American Medical Women's Association* 56 (2001), pp. 133–136.; David R. Williams, "Race, stress and mental health," in *Minority Health in America: Findings and Policy Implications from the Commonwealth Fund Minority Health Survey*, eds. C. Houge, M.A. Hargraves and K.S. Collins (Baltimore: Johns Hopkins University Press, 2000), pp. 209–242.
191. B. McEwen and E. Stellar, "Stress and the individual: Mechanisms leading to disease," *Archives of Internal Medicine* 153, (1993), pp. 2093–2101.
192. Carl V. Hill, Harold W. Neighbors and Helene D. Gayle, "The Relationship Between Racial Discrimination and Health for Black Americans: Measurement Challenges and the Realities of Coping," *African American Research Perspectives* 10:1 (2004), pp. 89–98.
193. J. Rich-Edwards, N. Krieger, J. Majzoub, S. Zierler, E. Lieberman and M. Gillman, "Maternal experiences of racism and violence as predictors of preterm birth: Rationale and study design," *Paediatric Perinatal Epidemiology* 15 (supplement 2) (2001), pp. 124–135.
194. Arline T. Geronimus, Margaret Hicken, Danya Keene and John Bound, ""Weathering and Age Patterns of Allostatic Load Scores Among Blacks and Whites in the United States," *American Journal of Public Health* 96:5 (May, 2006), pp. 826–833.
195. Kathy Sanders-Phillips, Beverlyn Settles-Reaves, Doren Walker and Janeese Brownlow, "Social Inequality and Racial Discrimination: Risk Factors for Health Disparities in Children of Color," *Pediatrics* 124 (supplement November 2009), pp. 176–186, http://pediatrics.aappublications.org/cgi/content/full/124/Supplement_3/S176.
196. Blitstein (2009).
197. "Unnatural Causes: Is Inequality Making Us Sick?" California Newsreel documentary ("When The Bough Breaks" part one, transcript 2008), p. 6.
198. Luo (2009).
199. "Racism's Cognitive Toll: Subtle Discrimination Is More Taxing on the Brain," *ScienceDaily* (September 24, 2007), www.sciencedaily.com/releases/2007/09/070919093316.htm.
200. Nancy Krieger and Stephen Sidney MD, "Racial Discrimination and Blood Pressure: The CARDIA Study of Young Black and White Adults," *American Journal of Public Health* 86 (1996), pp. 1370–1378.
201. Blitstein (2009).
202. Brown et al. (2003), pp. 15, 46.
203. Elizabeth Cohen, "Does your doctor judge you based on your color?" *CNN Health.com* (July 26, 2009), www.cnn.com/2009/HEALTH/07/23/doctors.attitude.race.weight/index.html?iref=mpstoryview.

204. "Racism is Harmful to Your Mental Health," *Healthy Place.com* (accessed October 5, 2009), www.healthyplace.com/anxiety-panic/main/racism-is-harmful-to-your-mental-health/menu-id-69.
205. "Racial and Ethnic Disparities Detected in Patient Experiences," *ScienceDaily* (October 30, 2008), www.sciencedaily.com/releases/2008/10/081028184826.htm.
206. "Emergency treatment may be only skin deep," *ScienceDaily* (August 22, 2007), www.sciencedaily.com/releases/2007/08/070820112820.htm.
207. Brown et al. (2003), p. 48.
208. "Physicians' Implicit and Explicit Attitudes About Race by MD Race, Ethnicity and Gender," *Journal of Health Care for the Poor and Underserved* 20:3 (August, 2009).
209. Shavers and Shavers (2006), pp. 388, 390.
210. Shavers and Shavers (2006), p. 392.
211. L.N. Borrell, D.R. Jacobs Jr., D.R. Williams, M.J. Pletcher, T.K. Houston and C.I. Kiefe, "Self-reported racial discrimination and substance abuse in the Coronory Artery Risk Development in Adults Study," *American Journal of Epidemiology* 166 (2007), pp. 1068–1079; Y. Choi, T.W. Harachi, M.R. Gillmore and R.F. Catalano, "Are multicultural adolescents at greater risk? Comparisons of rates, patterns, and correlates of substance use and violence between monoracial and multiracial adolescents," *The American Journal of Orthopsychiatry* 76 (2006), pp. 86–97; H. Landrine and E.A. Klonoff, "Racial discrimination and cigarette smoking among blacks: Findings from two studies," *Ethnicity and Disease* 10 (2008), pp. 195–202.
212. Brown et al. (2003), p. 89.
213. United States Department of Commerce, Bureau of the Census, "Poverty in the United States, 2000," *Current Population Survey* (March, 2000).
214. Linda Burnham, "Welfare Reform, Family Hardship, and Women of Color," in *Lost Ground: Welfare Reform, Poverty and Beyond*, eds. Randy Albelda and Ann Withorn (Boston: South End Press, 2002), p. 50.
215. Dalton Conley, *Being Black, Living in the Red: Race, Wealth and Social Policy in America* (Berkeley, CA: University of California Press, 1999), pp. 61, 70–71.
216. Lucy Williams, *Decades of Distortion: The Right's 30-Year Assault on Welfare* (Somerville, MA: Political Research Associates, 1997), p. 14.
217. Fred L. Block, Richard A. Cloward, Barbara Ehrenreich and Frances Fox Piven, *The Mean Season: The Attack on the Welfare State* (New York: Pantheon, 1987), pp. 55–56.
218. Conley (1999), pp. 68, 72.
219. Carol Goodenow and Kathleen E. Grady, "The Relationship of School Belonging and Friends' Values to Academic Motivation Among Urban Adolescent Students," *Journal of Experimental Education* 62 (1993), pp. 60–71; Brenda Major and Toni Schmader, "Coping With Stigma Through Psychological Disengagement," in *Prejudice: The Target's Perspective*, eds. Janet K. Swim and Charles Stangor (New York: Academic Press, 1998), pp. 219–41; Kristin E. Voelkel, "Identification With School," *American Journal of Education* 105 (1997), pp. 294–318.
220. Philip J. Cook and Jens Ludwig, "Weighing the Burden of 'Acting White': Are There

Race Differences in Attitudes Towards Education?" *Journal of Policy Analysis and Management* 16:2 (Spring, 1997), pp. 256–78.

221. Massey et al. (2002), p. 9.
222. Sarah Carr, "Coalition Says Study Rebuts Education Myths: Responses Demonstrate Commitment of Minority Students, Educators Say," *Milwaukee Journal Sentinel Online* (November 19, 2002), www.jsonline.com/news/metro/nov02/97244; Catherine Gewertz, "No Racial Gap Seen in Students' School Outlook," *Education Week* (November 20, 2002).
223. Blau (2003), pp. 57–59, 84–85, 92–93.
224. U.S. Bureau of the Census, *Statistical Abstracts of the United States, 2007* (Washington, DC: Government Printing Office, 2007), Table 530, p. 349.
225. Conley (1999), p. 127.
226. Williams (1997), p. 2
227. Nancy Dowd, *In Defense of Single Parent Families* (New York: NYU Press, 1997), p. 100.
228. Katznelson (2005), pp. 14–15.
229. Algernon Austin, "Three lessons about black poverty," Economic Policy Institute (September 18, 2009), www.epi.org/authors/bio/austin_algernon.
230. Shapiro (2004), p. 49.
231. Ronald F. Ferguson, "Addressing Racial Disparity in High Achieving Suburban Schools," *NCREL Policy Issues* 13 (North Central Regional Educational Lab, December, 2002), www.ncrel.org/policy/pubs/html/pivol13/dec2002b.htm.
232. Lawrence D. Bobo and James R. Kluegel, "Opposition to Race Targeting: Self-Interest, Stratification, Ideology or Racial Attitudes?" *American Sociological Review* 58:4 (1993), pp. 443–64; Gilens (1999).
233. Martin Gilens, " 'Race Coding' and White Opposition to Welfare," *American Political Science Review* (1996), pp. 593–595.
234. Alberto Alesina, Edward Glaeser and Bruce Sacerdote, *Why Doesn't the US Have a European-Style Welfare State?* (Harvard Institute of Economic Research, Discussion Paper No. 1933, November 2001), http://post.economics.harvard.edu/hier/2001papers/2001list.html.
235. Blasi (2008), p. 59
236. Ismail K. White, "When Race Matters and When It Doesn't: Racial Group Differences in Response to Racial Cues," *American Political Science Review* 101:2 (May 2007), p. 340.
237. Marc J. Hetherington and Jonathan D. Weiler, "Health Care, Race and Political Polarization," *Washington Post* (September 21, 2009), http://voices.washingtonpost.com/shortstack/2009/09/health_care_race_and_political.html.
238. Tom Jacobs, "I'd Like the Same Plan Better If It Was Bill Clinton's," *Miller-McCune News Blog* (November 13, 2009), http://miller-mccune.com/news/id-like-the-same-plan-better-if-it-was-bill-clintons-1608; Eric D. Knowles, Brian S. Lowery and Rebecca L. Schaumberg, "Racial prejudice predicts opposition to Obama and his health care reform plan," *Journal of Experimental Social Psychology* (2009),

www.sciencedirect.com/science?_ob=ArticleURL&_udi=B6WJB-4XKXXWC-1&_user=10&_rdoc=1&_fmt=&_orig=search&_sort=d&_docanchor=&view=c&_acct=C000050221&_version=1&_urlVersion=0&_userid=10&md5=90796b2b5343623c734c53c9ad53ba65.

239. Ismail K. White (2007), p. 348.
240. Even more bizarre than the reparations claim, Beck has warned his audience that racial shakedowns are just around the corner if the President's health care proposal passes, because the Office of Minority Health might allow for "litigation against Doritos," since people of color may "eat more Doritos." That the Office of Minority Health has been around since 1986 and has never sought to sue or encourage litigation against the makers of tortilla chips matters not to Beck, apparently. Media Matters for America, "Beck: 'Office of Minority Health' could allow for 'litigation against Doritos' since 'minorities' may 'eat more Doritos' " (July 24, 2009), http://mediamatters.org/print/clips/200907240012.
241. Serwer (2009).
242. Media Matters for America, "Limbaugh: America is 'so multicultured and fractured' that it 'may be two or three different countries'" (September 11, 2009), http://mediamatters.org/print/clips/200909110020.
243. Media Matters for America, "Limbaugh attacks 'the left' for 'celebrating diversity' and ending the 'distinct American culture'" (September 14, 2009), http://mediamatters.org/print/clips/200909140019.
244. Joe Conason, "Crackpots calling the kettle black," *Salon.com* (June 5, 2009), www.salon.com/opinion/conason/2009/06/05/sotomayor/print.html.
245. *Daily Kos TV* (May 29, 2009), www.dailykostv.com/w/001800.
246. Media Matters for America (July 23, 2009), http://mediamatters.org/print/clips/200907230019.
247. Media Matters for America (July 24, 2009), http://mediamatters.org/print/clips/200907240015.
248. Adam Winkler, "Obama was Right About the Gates Arrest," *Huffington Post* (July 25, 2009), www.huffingtonpost.com/adam-winkler/obama-was-right-about-the_b_244888.html.
249. "Fox Host Glenn Beck: Obama is a 'Racist' " (video), *Huffington Post* (July 28, 2009), www.huffingtonpost.com/2009/07/28/fox-host-glenn-beck-obama_n_246310.html?view=print.
250. Media Matters for America, "Limbaugh: 'In Obama's America, the white kids now get beat up with the black kids cheering' " (September 15, 2009), http://mediamatters.org/mmtv/200909150017.
251. "Limbaugh: Adolf Hitler, Like Barack Obama, Ruled by Dictate" (audio), *Huffington Post* (August 6, 2009), www.huffingtonpost.com/2009/08/06/limbaugh-adolf-hitler-lik_n_253412.html.
252. Media Matters for America, "Rush Limbaugh's obsession with Nazi comparisons," (August 7, 2009), http://mediamatters.org/print/blog/200908070035.
253. Eric Boehlert, "Glenn Beck and the rise of Fox News' militia media" (April 7, 2009), http://mediamatters.org/columns/200904070009.

254. Media Matters for America, "Limbaugh: 'Obama's entire economic program is reparations' " (July 22, 2009), http://mediamatters.org/mmtv/200907220040.
255. Media Matters for America, "Limbaugh: Obama is 'more African in his roots than he is American' and is 'behaving like an African colonial despot' " (June 26, 2009), http://mediamatters.org/mmtv/200906260019.
256. "Indonesian Muslim turned welfare thug," "Racist in Chief," www.marktalk.com/blog/?p=7204.
257. "Free Republic Pulls/Restores/Pulls Thread Bashing Malia Obama; FR Responds," *DailyKos* (July 10, 2009), www.dailykos.com/story/2009/7/10/752031/-*UPDATE-III*-Free-Republic-Pulls-Restores-Pulls-Thread-Bashing-Malia-Obama;-FR-Responds.
258. John Avlon, "New GOP 'Racist' Headache," *The Daily Beast* (July 6, 2009), www.thedailybeast.com/blogs-and-stories/2009-07-06/new-gop-racist-headache/p/. Interestingly, when some of Shay's other Republican friends complained about the racist post and her reply to it, which had been to say "You tell 'em Eric! LOL," she defriended the ones *who complained* rather than the racist who made the original posting.
259. Ben Hoover, "GOP activist says escaped gorilla was 'ancestor' of Michelle Obama," *WIS News 10* (Columbia, SC), June 12, 2009. www.wistv.com/Global/story.asp?s=10526195&clienttype=printable
260. John Amato, "Dr. David McKalip—Mr. Tea-Party—forwards racist Obama pic," *Crooks and Liars* (July 24, 2009), http://crooksandliars.com/node/29912.
261. Oliver Willis, "Racism on Display in Anti-Health Care Rallies" (August 4, 2009), www.oliverwillis.com/2009/08/04/racism-on-display-in-anti-health-care-rallies.
262. www.flickr.com/photos/jr1882/3793137116.
263. "Teabagger wit: Lyin' African," *Democratic Underground* (September 14, 2009), www.democraticunderground.com/discuss/duboard.php?az=view_all&address=389x6543413.
264. "The McCaskill Town Hall Incident: told from every angle," www.citizentube.com/2009/08/mccaskill-town-hall-incident-told-from.html.
265. "Obama Chides Holder for Comments on Race," *Huffington Post* (March 7, 2009), www.huffingtonpost.com/2009/03/07/obama-chides-holder-for-c_n_172771.html.
266. Michael Russnow, "Obama Backtracks Calling Police Action Stupid: Was It Moderation or Is Obama Becoming the First Wimp?" *Huffington Post* (July 25, 2009), www.huffingtonpost.com/michael-russnow/obama-backtracks-calling_b_244794.html.
267. Steve Holland, "Obama disagrees with Jimmy carter on race issue," *Reuters* (September 16, 2009), www.reuters.com/articlePrint?articleId=USTRE58F5NX20090916.
268. Jim Sleeper, *Liberal Racism* (New York: Viking Press, 1994), p. 177.
269. John A. Powell, "Obama's Universal Approach Leaves Many Excluded," *Huffington Post* (December 11, 2009), www.huffingtonpost.com/john-a-powell/obamas-universal-approach_b_389147.html.
270. Warren (forthcoming, 2010).

271. Jody Armour, "Stereotypes and Prejudice: Helping Legal Decisionmakers Break the Prejudice Habit," *California Law Review* 83 (1995), p. 733.
272. Armour (1995). The full transcript of Darrow's closing argument to the jury in the Henry Sweet trial can be read at www.law.umkc.edu/faculty/projects/ftrials/sweet/darrowsummation.html#I%20Say%20You%20Are.
273. Armour (1995), p. 733.
274. Blasi (2008), p. 45.
275. Samuel R. Sommers and Omoniyi O. Adekanmbi, "Race and Juries: An Experimental Psychology Perspective," in *Critical Race Realism* (2008), p. 81.
276. Sommers and Adekanmbi (2008), p. 85.
277. Armour (1995).
278. Drew Westen, "How Race Turns Up the Volume on Incivility: A Scientifically Informed Post-Mortem to a Controversy," *Huffington Post* (September 23, 2009), www.huffingtonpost.com/drew-westen/how-race-turns-up-the-vol_b295874.html.
279. Patricia G. Devine, "Stereotypes and Prejudice: Their Automatic and Controlled Components," *Journal of Personality and Social Psychology* 56 (1989), pp. 5–6.
280. Patricia G. Devine, Ashby E. Plant, David M. Amodio, Eddie Harmon-Jones and Stephanie L. Vance, "The regulation of explicit and implicit race bias: The role of motivations to respond without prejudice," *Journal of Personality and Social Psychology* 82:5 (2002), pp. 835—48.
281. Philip Mazzocco, *The Dangers of Not Speaking About Race: A Summary of Research Affirming the Merits of a Color-Conscious Approach to Racial Communication and Equity* (Columbus, OH: The Kirwan Institute for the Study of Race and Ethnicity, Ohio State University, May 2006), p. 7.
282. Debra Van Ausdale and Joe R. Feagin, *The First R: How Children Learn Race and Racism* (New York: Rowman and Littlefield, 2002).
283. Po Bronson and Ashley Merryman, *NurtureShock* (New York: Twelve Books, 2009), pp. 54–55.
284. Bronson and Merryman (2009).
285. For information on antiracist resistance, and especially white allyship in the antiracist struggle, see, Herbert Aptheker, *Anti-Racism in U.S. History: The First Two Hundred Years* (Westport, CT: Praeger Publishers, 1993).
286. C.B. Fisher, S.A. Wallace and R.E. Fenton, "Discrimination distress during adolescence," *Journal of Youth and Adolescence* 20:6 (2000), pp. 679–695.
287. Clark McKown and Michael Strambler, "Developmental Antecedents and Social and Academic Consequences of Stereotype-Consciousness in Middle Childhood," *Child Development* 80:6 (November, 2009), pp. 1643–1659, http://www3.interscience.wiley.com/journal/122683307/abstract.
288. "Fear of Messing Up May Undermine Interracial Contact," *ScienceDaily* (April 2, 2008), www.sciencedaily.com/releases/2008/04/080401161614.htm.
289. Evan P. Apfelbaum, Samuel R. Sommers and Michael I. Norton, "Seeing race and seeming racist? Evaluating strategic colorblindness in social interaction," *Journal of Personality and Social Psychology* 95:4 (2008), p. 918.

290. Sommers and Adekanmbi (2008), 88.
291. William E. Sedlacek, "Why we should use noncognitive variables with graduate and professional students," *The Advisor: The Journal of the National Association of Advisors for the Health Professions*. 24:2 (2004), pp. 32–39; Terence J. Tracey and William E. Sedlacek, "A comparison of white and black student academic success using noncognitive variables: A LISREL analysis," *Research in Higher Education* 27:4 (December, 1987), pp. 333–348.
292. Carol Corbett Burris, Kevin G. Welner and Jennifer Weiser Bezoza, "Universal Access to Quality Education: Research and Recommendations for the Elimination of Curricular Stratification," *Poverty and Race* 19:1 (Poverty and Race Research Council, January/February 2010), p. 3.
293. Claude M. Steele, "A Threat in the Air: How Stereotypes Shape Intellectual Identity and Performance," *American Psychologist* 52 (1997), p. 613–629.
294. Philip Uri Treisman, "A Practitioner's View From Texas," in *Promise and Dilemma: Perspectives on Racial Diversity in Higher Education*, ed. Eugene Y. Lowe, Jr. (Princeton, NJ: Princeton University Press, 1999), p. 129–132; "A Teacher Had a Question: Lessons Learned from FIPSE Projects II—September 1993," http://vccslitonline.cc.va.us/MRCTE/treisman.htm.
295. "Middle School Math Classes are Key to Closing Racial Achievement Gap," *ScienceDaily* (April 22, 2009), www.sciencedaily.com/releases/2009/04/090420121433.htm.
296. David E. Drew, *Aptitude Revisited: Rethinking Math and Science Education for America's Next Century* (Baltimore, MD: Johns Hopkins University Press, 1996).
297. Steele (1997).
298. Geoffrey L. Cohen, Julio Garcia, Valerie Purdie-Vaughns, Nancy Apfel and Patricia Brzustoski, "Recursive Processes in Self-Affirmation: Intervening to Close the Minority Achievement Gap," *Science* 324 (April 17, 2009), p. 400–403.
299. Geoffrey L. Cohen, Julio Garcia, Nancy Apfel and Allison Master, "Reducing the Racial Achievement Gap: A Social-Psychological Intervention," *Science* 313 (September 1, 2006), p. 1307–1310.
300. Susan Greene, "Stark Stats Motivate Black Kids," *Denver Post* (December 30, 2007,) www.denverpost.com/search/ci_7839013.
301. Theresa Perry, "Freedom for Literacy and Literacy for Freedom: The African American Philosophy of Education," in *Young, Gifted and Black: Promoting High Achievement Among African American Students*, eds. Theresa Perry, Claude Steele and Asa Hilliard III (Boston: Beacon Press, 2003), pp. 11–51.

ABOUT THE AUTHOR

Tim Wise is among the nation's most prominent writers and educators on issues of racial justice. He is the author of four previous books on racism and has contributed essays or chapters to more than twenty additional volumes. Wise has spoken to hundreds of thousands of persons on more than 750 college and high school campuses across the United States and has trained teachers, employers, nonprofit agencies, physicians and others on methods for dismantling racism in their institutions. He has appeared on hundreds of radio and television programs to discuss racial issues, and his writings are taught in colleges and universities worldwide. Wise lives in Nashville with his wife and two daughters.

RECENT AND FORTHCOMING
FROM THE OPEN MEDIA SERIES

The Black History of the White House
by Clarence Lusane

Narrative of the Life of Frederick Douglass, An American Slave
A New Critical Edition
by Angela Y. Davis

New World of Indigenous Resistance:
Noam Chomsky and Voices from North, South, and Central America
Edited by Lois Meyer, Benjamín Maldonado

Dying to Live: A Story of U.S. Immigration in an Age of Global Apartheid
by Joseph Nevins and Mizue Aizeki

A Power Governments Cannot Suppress
by Howard Zinn

Making the Future: The Unipolar Imperial Moment
by Noam Chomsky

OPEN MEDIA SERIES

Open Media is a movement-oriented publishing project committed to the vision of "one world in which many worlds fit"—a world with social justice, democracy, and human rights for all people. Founded during wartime in 1991 by Greg Ruggiero, Open Media has a history of producing critically acclaimed and best-selling titles that address the most urgent political and social issues of our time.

City Lights Books |www.citylghts.com